"This is wonderful! This is the direction which culture in our world should take: to make stories and songs meaningful within every family, every people!"
—PETE SEEGER

"Rosenbluth gives an eloquent rationale for the value of sharing family stories with future generations—from understanding one's ethnic heritage, giving family members a sense of identity with the past, to the simple desire for communication in an era when generations often live many miles apart and do not have the benefit of daily conversation."
—*Northwest Oral History Association Newsletter*

"Very well written, easy to understand, and based on sound oral history technique."
—LINDA MORTON-KEITHLEY, Oral Historian, Idaho State Historical Society

"A small gem of common sense uncommonly well employed. Her instructions for would-be family interviewers (and their quarry) are simple, direct, and thorough."
—*Quill & Quire*

"… I read your book *Keeping Family Stories Alive* … I want you to know what an inspiration you have been to me and to my business partner in Roots & Wings Life Stories.
—AUDREY GALEX, Roots & Wings Life Stories

"I believe that this book would be the ideal handbook for anyone who wanted to get started.… the philosophy and the practical suggestions are relevant to anybody wanting to interview members of the older generation. I found particularly useful the discussion about the nature of memory, as well as the chapter addressed to the potential interviewee, someone who everybody else has tended to overlook."
—ROGER KITCHEN, General Manager,
The Living Archive Project, Stantonbury Campus, England

"Given the growing interest in family history and family stories and the paucity of high quality how-to manuals on interviewing and recording family members, [*Keeping Family Stories Alive*] fills a real need in the field."
—BARBARA ALLEN, Associate Professor, *University of Notre Dame,
Department of American Studies*

"With the growing interest in genealogy and family history, this guide is timely. Along with the methodology it offers, it has the potential to enrich and broaden family research. For practitioners in the wider field of oral history, it provides a refreshing sensitivity to the interview process that cannot help but refine one's awareness and approach to oral history."   —*Archives of BC, Victoria*

"… a delightful 'do-it-yourself' book. Rosenbluth writes with such enthusiasm and clarity that the reader recognizes that recording family history is not only desirable and pleasurable, but can also lead to greater mutual appreciation and understanding between generations."
—*BC Library Association Reporter* Vol 35, no. 2

"If you are the hopeful archivist of your family's lore, this book will nourish your ability to handle every aspect for the task—preparing for interviews (tips for both asker and askee), recording them (both audio and video), preserving the tapes. A most unusual, and unusually helpful, book.
—*Whole Earth Millennium*

"… a primer for preserving the uniqueness of a family as well as a persuasive argument for capturing what only past generations can offer."
—1991, HARRY F. ROSENTHAL, "Over 50"- Associated Press

"*Keeping Family Stories Alive* is as much devoted to inspiring readers to record family stories as it is to sharing advice on how to conduct the interview."
—*Vision Magazine* (The Loen Group)

KEEPING
FAMILY STORIES ALIVE

Keeping Family Stories Alive

DISCOVERING AND RECORDING THE
STORIES AND REFLECTIONS
OF A LIFETIME

SECOND EDITION

VERA ROSENBLUTH

Illustrations by Rae Maté

Hartley & Marks
PUBLISHERS

Published by
HARTLEY & MARKS PUBLISHERS INC.
P. O. Box 147   3661 West Broadway
Point Roberts, WA   Vancouver, BC
98281   V6R 2B8

LIBRARY OF CONGRESS CATALOGING-IN-PUBLICATION DATA
Rosenbluth, Vera.
Keeping family stories alive : discovering and recording the stories and
reflections of a lifetime / by Vera Rosenbluth. —Rev. ed.
p.   cm.
Includes bibliographical references and index.
ISBN 0-88179-149-0
1. Genealogy. 2. Oral biography. 3. Sound—Recording and
reproducing. 4. Video recordings—Production and direction.
5. Interviewing. I. Title.
CS21.R574   1997
929.1—dc21   97-10683
CIP

Design and composition by The Typeworks
Cover design by Diane McIntosh
Back cover photo by Lisl Ponger

Set in BEMBO

Printed in the U.S.A.

For my parents, Mimi and Gideon Rosenbluth,
who gave me a rich treasury of family stories.
And for my sons, Marc and Jonathan,
who will value those stories and contribute
many new ones of their own.

CONTENTS

FOREWORD
by Ruth Edmonds Hill

You are opening a new door—a door into oral history, especially as it relates to collecting family stories. You may already know the stories fully or in part, but you can have the pleasure of collecting them and preserving them for the enjoyment of other family members. This book will be your guide.

What is oral history and why is it particularly useful for the process of collecting family stories?

At one time, all history was collected and passed down orally through the generations. This is still true in some cultures. In a paper presented before the Society of American Archivists annual meeting, I said, "Oral history … is a casualty and paradoxically a beneficiary of technology. The invention of the printing press (by Johannes Gutenberg around 1450 AD), and with it the ability to compile a bibliographic record and to preserve it, assisted in the death of this kind of oral history. The new oral history is a beneficiary of the invention of first the wire recorder, then the tape recorder, the cassette tape, and even videotape." By the middle of the nineteenth century, historians were essentially studying only written documents, and were no longer speaking with a living informant. In school I studied declarations of war between nations, and the peace treaties. I learned about people, primarily men, considered important historically. But I learned nothing of the everyday lives of the citizens. On CNN (Cable News Network) which brings news from around the world 24 hours a day, we look at disasters—man-made and natural—and the people involved, but we learn very little of their physical conditions, or emotional feelings and perceptions. Sometimes, the newscaster will interview an individual in order to round out the story. But these are only 30-second or one-minute "sound bites." Oral history, with its more leisurely pace, can provide a depth of understanding of an individual's experience. Oral history gives us a record of a person's perceptions and feelings about an event, which may be as important or as interesting as the event itself.

In 1948 Allan Nevins, writing about twentieth century New York City politics, discovered that there was insufficient written documentation available. He decided that interviews would be the best way to get the information he wanted. That was perhaps the beginning of a new wave of "oral" history—speaking with people who lived through the experiences we want to examine.

In my view, one reason that oral history has developed is that it is primary rather than secondary discourse. The teller is the authority and resource. The teller knows and has lived the story and can share his or her perceptions and life experiences directly—they do not have to be interpreted through a third person. Oral history is a democratic technique by which you may collect a person's life story and preserve it for your family and friends, and future generations.

Speaking from the point of view of a person born and brought up in the United States, I feel that the civil rights movement, anti-war movements, and the women's movement had a lot to do with the development of oral history and non-elite history. Groups wanted to tell their own stories and not leave them to authoritarian telling and interpretation by a professional historian, or by a member of another (perhaps controlling) race, sex, or ethnic group in the seats of power. Sometimes these stories have been in opposition to the generally accepted story.

In an article on the interplay of culture, history, and memory in the *Oral History Review*, William S. Schneider says:

> ... oral history provides clues to values—values that may be very different from those found in the written sources or even the types of evidence that are usually considered in debating the success or failure of an activity. Therefore it is historically important to ask people how they recall the past.

You may collect oral history material for its historical value alone, but there are other reasons for doing oral history. It might be used to help build a community, or to bring generations closer. And there is also the healing aspect which can take place not only in the narrator's life, but also in an entire family or between generations.

Oral history can be used to help build a new family or a community identity. There is no one definition of community. It can be any group of people. For example, the men and women in a nursing home all come from different places and have different life experiences. They now live together. How can they bridge the gaps? One way is through a particular kind of storytelling, i.e., the sharing of their life stories and experiences. Dr. Hugh Morgan Hill, a world-renowned storyteller known as Brother Blue, says, "If we knew each other's stories, we could no longer kill each other so easily. There would be no such thing as 'ethnic cleansing.' The whole world would become a family."

We are no longer three- or four-generation families living close together. Many of us gather only at weddings or funerals or family reunions. Take along your tape recorder and use these opportunities to collect family stories. Today's young people often do not have an opportunity to hear their elders' stories; whether personal life stories or stories about the "uncle who ran away to America," stories about family traditions, or the recipe for the "raspberry pie that always won first place at the fair." We seem not to value the life experiences and wisdom of our elders. An exchange of stories across the generations can be important in both directions. Although this can be done *en famille*, perhaps the best way for young people to do this is in a school project. Oral history is equally useful in the college classroom, supplementing the textbooks or documentary research, especially in areas such as gender and race or ethnicity issues. Again, the source material can be interviews with family members. As you do your project, either on your own or in the classroom, you will come to realize that history is not just what happened long ago and far away. It is still happening and you are part of it. I once came across an Arab proverb that says that every day of your life is a page of your history. All these individual pages and life stories make up what we call "history."

One of the projects under my care at the Schlesinger Library at Radcliffe College is the Black Women Oral History Project. Susie Williams Jones, interviewed in 1977, said:

> My oldest son died in 1976; for me he was a great support.... David Jr.'s death was a shattering experience and I have not been able to adjust yet to this. Yesterday opened doors, and for the first time I looked at my life as a whole.

You can see that all the stories you collect in your interviews will not be happy. Sometimes you will have to deal with sad experiences or even sensitive personal information. You will need to have patience in the situation and empathy for the person telling the story.

More and more, social historians are studying the lives of families and the individual, everyday person. At one time, family history was done only from genealogical records, the written documentation of a family, but oral history can provide texture to the story. Although you are collecting your oral history primarily for family use, you and family members may feel the interview is of sufficient historical interest or quality to donate it to a public institution, such as a library or a historical society.

N. Scott Momaday, of Kiowa heritage, in the book *Ancestral Voice* speaks of the many masks or identities he wears. A carefully structured interview can help to reveal the true person behind the masks. Therefore, you as the interviewer should do some preliminary research on the narrator's life in order to give some structure to the interview and help determine the questions to be asked. Other family members can help with their own stories. Looking at the family Bible, scrapbooks, and photographs can be both useful and fun.

Remember that another family member probably will get a completely different story. An interview is very much a function of the relationship between the interviewer and the narrator. And your interview is just a small and particular moment in the vast spectrum of time.

A life story oral history interview with an elder can give that person an opportunity to sum up his or her life. It is not to bring closure to the life, but it is an opportunity for review, for understanding his or her experiences. This summing up can be of value to the narrator. Susie Williams again:

> I am deeply grateful to the Radcliffe Committee who have given me this opportunity to gather myself together. Howard Thurman talks about the therapy of memory. My days with Dr. Tate [the interviewer] ... have been truly an adventure into the past, and I could not have done this without her constant patience and encouragement ... I have been greatly blessed to have gathered together my whole life.

Whether you collect a whole life story or some scattered episodes from a life, or tales about family traditions, it will have meaning for the narrator, for you as the interviewer, and for your family. Take it a step at a time. With this book in hand, just begin. You will enjoy it!

— RUTH EDMONDS HILL
Audiovisual Coordinator,
Schlesinger Library, Radcliffe College

PREFACE TO THE
SECOND EDITION

A wonderful thing often happens when people are asked to tell the stories of their lives. It was described effectively by writer Mary Lovell in the prologue to *Straight on Till Morning: The Biography of Beryl Markham*.

In the mid-1980s Lovell had heard that the legendary Markham, pioneer aviatrix and racehorse trainer, then in her eighties, was living a rather reclusive life in Kenya. Lovell decided that she wanted to write Markham's biography. Warned by several acquaintances that Markham was "difficult," that her mind was no longer clear, and that she had cut herself off from former friends, Mary Lovell began to build a relationship with her subject in order to research the book.

For a few weeks the writer visited Beryl Markham every day, bringing small gifts, going through papers and records, and asking her questions about her life. The writer soon realized that loneliness, boredom, and a lack of mental stimulation were the main causes of Markham's depression. The process of talking about her glamorous and adventurous past, of the famous people she had known, and reliving the excitement of being the first person to fly solo west to east across the Atlantic, brought new life to the elderly woman. Markham began taking an interest in her appearance once again, forced herself to leave her wheelchair and walk on her own, and insisted on being taken to the horseraces that she used to love. Beryl Markham acknowledged the effect that the process of remembering the past had on her in a short preface she wrote in 1986, just a few months before her death:

> Day after day, I have listened while she read these papers to
> me. I have remembered times long past and people long dead.
> And when she asked me I have tried to tell her about them.
> But some memories I have kept for myself as everyone must.

And because she understands this I have tried to help her, as she—in her own way—helped me.

Not all stories are this dramatic, of course, but since the publication of the first edition of this book, I have become more convinced than ever of the importance of interviewing people about their lives. As Mary Lovell and Beryl Markham found, as well as yielding previously untold stories and rich oral history, the process itself is a healing and validating one. I have received many letters from people telling me that they used the book as a guide to do tape recordings with their parents, and it delights me when they are pleased with the outcome. There have been poignant letters from people who conducted interviews with a parent who died shortly thereafter, and whose tapes are prized even more highly for being irreplaceable. And there have been many reports from people who developed a deeper understanding and appreciation of their parents or grandparents.

I have been gratified by the response to the book from ordinary people who are looking for a way to discover and present their own family stories, from elders who were excited and pleased to be asked for their stories, professional oral historians, teachers who use the techniques in their classrooms, and community groups who are engaged in local history projects. They have encouraged me to write the new material that I have included in this second edition and I am grateful for their suggestions.

At lectures and workshops where I talk about the value of conducting interviews with family members, and give some guidelines for how to go about it, one question invariably arises: How do I deal with family secrets? We are all fascinated by those shadowy figures and hazy incidents in our family history which are not talked about very much. I have added a chapter on family secrets in an attempt to navigate this hazardous area, trying to tread the line between acknowledging people's right to privacy and the sense of release that comes with unburdening oneself of weighty secrets.

Teachers who have invited me to their classes to talk about interviewing elders have suggested that I give some clear guidelines on undertaking an oral history project in a school setting. This is something that individual enterprising teachers do all over the continent, but there are few common resources for them to use. I hope that teachers find the new chapter useful in their work, as well as in their own families.

Frequently, when I try to explain my fascination with family stories, people say, "Oh, you're interested in genealogy." Of course it's not the same thing, but it is related. I've tried to talk about the relationship between genealogy and family stories in the third new chapter of this second edition, and to explore ways that genealogists can use the stories and the interviewing techniques to expand their research into family history. Since writing the first edition of this book, I have become intrigued by the idea of the genogram, a multi-generational chart that can contain a great deal of information about individual characteristics, relationships, and recurring patterns in a family. Using some simple guidelines, I have adapted this therapeutic tool for use in family story interviews, and suggested how it can replace the more conventional family tree or pedigree chart.

I remain convinced that the telling and hearing of life stories is an activity that connects, informs, validates, and entertains us, all at the same time. In the past few years there has been noticeable growth of interest in family stories, as reflected in novels, films, and even the development of a new generation of professional personal biographers. I am deeply honored that Ruth Hill, as much a "woman of courage" as those in her collection of oral histories of Black American women, has written a foreword for this second edition. I hope that the book moves you, the reader, to think about discovering and recording the stories of your own family, and that it gives you the confidence to begin. Please let me know how it goes for you!

V.R.
August 23, 1997

ACKNOWLEDGMENTS

I would like to express my warmest thanks to many people who helped me in the writing of this book:

to storytellers Mary Love May, Cathryn Wellner, Jan Andrews, Alice Kane, Joan Bodger, and Jane Yolen who shared their enthusiasm for family stories;

to Vicki Gabereau for her enthusiasm for this project from the beginning;

to Maria LeRose, Dolly Hannay, Roland LeRose, Gladys Martin, Elaine Wynne, Gillian Chetty, C. S. Boatwright, Spencer Baird, Kurt Weinberg, Gordon Bailey, Judith Schott, and Elvins Spencer, for their willingness to talk about their own experiences with me;

to David Suzuki, Fergus Craik, I. A. Bell, Jock Abra, for their conversations with me about how human memory works;

to Gary Johnson and Derek Reimer for making sure that the technical information in this book is accurate;

to Claire Moss and Joy Wild who believe in the importance of oral history projects in schools;

to Molly Moss, Hildegard Westerkamp, Pat Carfra, Diane Eaton, Georgia Earles, Adam Waldie, Ann Bailey and many other good friends whose continued interest and helpful comments have meant a great deal to me;

to my aunts Raja Rosenbluth and Hanna Spencer for all the stories they have told me;

thanks also to Rae Maté for her evocative drawings;

particular acknowledgment to two perceptive editors who see both the big picture and the smallest detail: Sue Tauber for the first edition, and Susan Juby for the second. Thanks as well to the rest of the staff at Hartley & Marks, who have made the writing of this book such a pleasure; and, as ever, special thanks to my husband Robin Hanvelt for his unfailing support.

xvii

A PROLOGUE OF SORTS...

Family stories are about the big issues we seldom discuss in our everyday lives: birth and death, love and friendship, joy and sorrow, success and failure, regret, anger, jealousy, pride, suffering and triumph, laughter and tears. They blend philosophies, memories, and insights in a way that is healing for both the teller and the listener.

When we ask questions of our parents or of others important in our lives, we recognize the commonality of the human experience, and come to understand the ways in which we are similar, as well as ways in which we differ. When telling our real-life stories, we gain an understanding of how all the fragmentary memories and isolated incidents fit together in our lives. In fact, we see that our lives are a story in which we are the hero, that we have come from somewhere, and that our lives have direction and purpose.

Family stories tell us about self-reliance and human interdependence, about individual uniqueness and family continuity, and, above all, about the remarkable resilience of the human spirit. They deserve to be recorded and remembered.

The Value of Telling and Hearing Family Stories

I have no money to leave to my grandchildren.
My stories are my wealth.

—ANGELA SIDNEY

We live in a remarkable age in which information and entertainment are available in overwhelming abundance through all the media that surround us. Yet, ironically, over the last generation or so, we have become less and less in touch with the histories and legends of our own particular families.

Sometimes it is not until a parent or grandparent dies that we realize just how little we know about our family history. And then, of course, it is too late to ask. That's why it's important to make the time to ask questions of our elders while we have the opportunity. It's an activity that has incalculable benefits for the older person who tells the stories of his or her life, as well as for the younger person who hears them. And if the conversation between them is taped on audio

For most people, the telling of a family story is best done in an interaction between two people.

or videotape, the permanent record will be valued by future generations as well.

Doing interviews with older people about their lives is a satisfying process which honors them by the very fact that someone is interested enough in them to want to know their stories. A young woman wrote to me after I had completed an interview with her mother: "You have no idea what a rewarding, positive, ego-boosting process this has been for my mother. Since my dad died, some of her current friends seem to treat her in a patronizing way. Her self-confidence as an intelligent, worthwhile person has been shaken. You and the whole story-telling process have breathed new life, new confidence and new strength into my mum."

Somewhere along the way, we have lost the art of telling family stories within our daily lives. Children used to grow up simply absorbing information about their families, knowing the stories and passing them on to their own children when they in turn became parents. But today many adults know surprisingly little about their own family history, or about the lives their parents led. So what has happened? Why have we lost this precious legacy? Why do we no longer tell our stories to our children and grandchildren? Why do so few people even know the names of their great-grandparents, let alone anything real or human about them?

The first and most obvious explanation is the changing pattern of families in our time. In previous generations it was common for people to live their entire lives in the same community; three or even four generations of a family would live in the same region. It used to be that stability was the most dependable feature of the social landscape; now change is the norm. Our mobile lifestyle has spread families across the country, and with increasing frequency, across the oceans. While children and their grandparents may have close and loving visits, they rarely have day-to-day contact with one another. There is, therefore, far less opportunity for the telling of family stories within the context of daily life than there used to be. Families are changing in other ways as well: a greater geographical distance often results in (or is the result of) greater emotional distance between the generations. The rising number of single parent families means that children are frequently estranged from one side of their family and know very little about one part of their heritage.

Traditionally it was an older person, often a grandparent, who took on the role of storyteller within the family. And in many societies, grandparents are indeed valued for their wisdom and experience, which they pass on to their grandchildren. But our society puts a great deal of emphasis on youth, and tends to ignore or stereotype older people. Rather than feeling valued, they are made to feel out of date in a world that is changing rapidly. Typically, young people feel that their grandparents don't have anything to teach them. I'll always remember a retired labor leader who had a vivid memory and a colorful way of telling labor stories of the 1930s. He had tried to tell these stories to his grandchildren, but their attitude was, "Oh, there goes Grandpa again with those old stories." It wasn't until the children saw their grandfather being interviewed on television that they started to pay attention! But many more older people take their stories with them when they die, because they think nobody cares to hear them.

These attitudes change as we get older and have children of our own. People in their thirties and forties, whose children are growing up without knowing much about their background, are becoming interested in asking their parents questions while they still can. I know a woman who left her native England as soon as she graduated from school to travel around the world. Her voyage was interrupted in Canada when she met the man she was to marry, and she settled there to raise a family. But as her children grew older, she realized that they knew very little about their grandparents and the world in which she herself had grown up. The family wasn't wealthy enough to travel frequently, so they had seen their grandparents very rarely. It occurred to her that she was the only link between their lives in

Interviewing older people about their lives honors them and their experiences.

3

Canada and their English heritage. Then her mother became ill and she decided to return to England for a visit. This time, however, she took a tape recorder along to record some of the family stories before it was too late.

Especially in North America, so many of the stories of our parents and grandparents are dramatic stories of immigration from other countries; stories that are particularly valuable for the succeeding generations to know in order to understand their ethnic heritage. Yet in the effort to assimilate and make a new life, in the day-to-day struggle to get ahead, these stories are often neglected or pushed aside. Quite simply, we often don't value the family stories enough to make the time to ask for them or to tell them.

Time is a key element in the telling of stories. When you value an activity, you have to make the time for it. But we live in an age when life seems to zip past at a frenetic pace. Our days are full, and our time is fragmented, fractured. The demands on our time seem constant. So when do we stop and make the time to reflect about our lives, to ask questions of our parents, to think about how we became who we are? When do we make the time to tell our children what we were like when we were their age? Even people who recognize the value of writing or recording their memoirs tend to put it off—partly because it seems like an intimidating task, partly because other, more immediately pressing, things interfere. Many people vow to write their memoirs when they retire. But modern retirees are often just as busy and active as they were when they were younger.

It is clear that remembering, recollecting our memories has to be done in calm and tranquil surroundings. When our lives are full of demands on our time, constant distractions and busy-ness, that time and space is not readily available to us. Any kind of creative work, be it art, writing, academic research, or reminiscing, requires some degree of peace and tranquility. A composer once remarked on the constant noise and sound that is part of the urban soundscape in the form of muzak, traffic, and other city sounds. She said that it is in the wilder-

ness, when she is free from the external voices of the city, that she has room to find her own musical voice and when she is most creative. Similarly, reflecting on the past requires special effort and quiet.

There are other factors in this trend toward the devaluing of family stories. One of the most significant is the ubiquitous television. The television set has replaced the grandparent as the family storyteller; time spent in front of the television set has replaced family time spent in conversation, reminiscing, and swapping yarns from the old days. And the glamorized, artificial images we see on television often have very little to do with our own lives. There is a wonderful tale beloved by storytellers about a primitive tribe in Africa which was being studied by an anthropologist. The anthropologist decided to introduce a television into tribal life and observe the effect of this modern wonder. All activity stopped, and people gathered around the electronic box for a few weeks. But gradually they drifted away until no one was watching the television. The anthropologist was puzzled, until one of the tribesmen said, "Well, we have our own storyteller." "Yes," said the anthropologist, "but the TV knows many more stories than your storyteller." "That may be true," replied the tribesman, "but our storyteller knows us."

Cultural philosophers and educators warn us that television is resulting in the "McBraining" of our lives; we are being kept amused and distracted, but in a passive and superficial way. Watching television is not a particularly creative activity. Our language becomes impoverished, our emotions trivialized, our sense of our own lives diminished. If we see our own lives as less glamorous or less exciting than those of the media stars, we are not likely to value the stories of our own family enough to ask about them.

So what is the value of telling family stories? Why does it matter what kind of people our grandparents were, what their lives were like, why our parents chose the professions they did, how they met each other, and so on? How does it affect our lives and why should we care about the past? Certainly in terms of making a living, under-

5

standing world events, keeping fit, or being concerned about the environment, family stories don't seem to have much to do with our daily lives. But they have everything to do with our sense of identity, our sense of roots, our sense of connectedness.

One of the joys of my childhood was listening to the stories that my grandmother would tell about her life in Czechoslovakia. She always referred to her homeland as "The Old Country," and to me that magical land existed only in her stories and my imagination. She came to North America just before the Second World War, when she was 50 years old, and I never visited the small village where she grew up. But through her stories I knew what it looked like, who the village "characters" were, how the landscape changed with the seasons. In particular, I had a vivid mental image of my grandmother as a small girl, understood what delighted her, what made her laugh, what frightened or distressed her, and what traits she and I shared.

The stories of my grandmother's life weren't especially unusual; every family has similar stories. But for me they were the most special stories in the world, because they were the stories of my family. Of course, the times my grandmother told them were ones of warmth and closeness. The details of life long ago, and in a faraway country, fascinated me in almost the same way as fairy tales and other bedtime stories. But these weren't fairy tales; they were true stories about real people. And because those real people were my ancestors, they made me feel special and connected. In effect, they laminated me into my own and my family's past, and were an important part of my sense of identity.

A ring which I wear belonged to a great-grandmother whom I know through these stories; this ring connects me to a courageous, compassionate, and independent woman. A set of dishes which my parents bring out on special occasions was brought along when the family had to hurriedly leave Czechoslovakia before World War II. Paintings, photos, embroidered tablecloths—all are infused with meaning and value by the stories that surround them.

As an adult, I realize now that my grandmother had as great a need to tell these stories as I had pleasure in hearing them. My attention and interest made her value her stories more, and therefore her life. Telling them to someone who cared about them gave shape and meaning to a life, which took her from a small European village to a large North American city, and spanned 80 years of change and flux. And although she died 20 years ago, the images and emotions evoked by her stories ensure that an essential part of her lives on.

By "storytelling," I mean simply the telling of anecdotes, happenings, the events of a person's life. Storytelling is the basic way we have always communicated with each other; based on memory and language, it is what sets us apart from other animals. Even the youngest child relates the day's adventures in the form of a story.

Stories give shape to the events and emotions that make up our lives. And they provide a sense of permanence, a way of remembering what has happened to us. Without stories, we lose our sense of the past and its connection to our present and future. Just as an amnesiac who has no memory of his past has lost the sense of who he is, so do we need stories from our past to give us a sense of our own identity.

Within families, stories passed on from one generation to the next solidify everyone's sense of belonging. Not only are they entertaining, but they also tell about genealogy, and the values and unique qualities of that particular family. They are real-life, sometimes exaggerated anecdotes told within a family to make a certain point. Family stories that come down through the generations are often ones of overcoming obstacles, and of courage and survival, and these can be inspiring in our own lives.

This is not to say that all family stories are inspiring or even happy. Many tell of struggle, tragedy, pain, and loss. But families tend to tell those stories that reinforce the values they hold and reinforce the image they have developed of themselves. My mother's mother's mother, whose ring I wear, was a young widow with three daughters. She owned a store in their small village in Czechoslovakia. The

most vivid story I know about her is of the time the men went on strike against the exploitive coal mine owners. My great-grandmother extended unlimited credit to them all to enable them to survive, and helped them in their labor negotiations; the success of the strike, one of the first in labor history, was largely due to her generosity. I grew up in a family which values a social conscience and awareness of injustice, and this story reinforces those ideals. So in one sense it's "just a story," but in another, it provides me with a model, invisible to anyone outside the family, of how to act in the world.

The telling of family stories used to happen very naturally. Children working or playing alongside their elders would spark reminiscences; family dinners or get-togethers were occasions for the recounting of family stories. Joking, laughing, and teasing about events in the past used to be a feature of community and family events such as quilting bees and Christmas cooking. Often the stories were told and retold many times, sometimes to the chagrin of the subject of those stories. It was common that grandparents lived in the same house as their grandchildren, or just down the street, or across town, and the stories were passed naturally from one generation to the next. Bedtime tales were as likely to come from real life as from books. The result was that children simply grew up with their family stories. This bonded them to their families and gave them the sense of being a link in a strong chain of kinship.

A woman in her late seventies who grew up on a rural homestead remembers the long winter evenings when she was a child, before the age of television, when friends of her parents would drop in to play cards and trade stories. She says she was never far from the table when they were talking! The stories were ones of humor, courage, and the pioneering spirit, and were always a source of strength to her. They were a lifeline connecting her to her past; and now she passes those same stories on to her own grandchildren—embellished a little, perhaps.

These grandchildren, although they probably don't realize it, are very fortunate. Changing family patterns, people moving away from

the community that knew them, a fast-paced life that doesn't leave time for reflection, a feeling of being isolated in a hectic mass society—all this means that older people rarely have the occasion of telling the stories of their lives to the children. And yet, we can't afford to wait for an occasion that might never come.

Fortunately, we can create the opportunity for telling family stories with a simple interview, most often one between two family members, the "teller" and the "interviewer." The role of the interviewer is to ask questions, to listen, and to record. The role of the teller is to delve into his or her past and share memories in response to the questions. Surely we value our own histories enough to tell them, and conversely, surely we care enough to ask questions of our elders before it is too late.

What it means to the teller

As we grow older, we experience a real need to "story" events from our past, to reminisce, to put events into the context of our entire lives. It's generally a pleasant activity that reminds us that our lives have been worthwhile. After taping an interview, one woman in her eighties remarked, "It made me feel as though it was all played out in front of me again." Even when one has experienced pain and suffering—and who hasn't?—giving voice to those parts of one's life years later can be cathartic.

But it can't be done in isolation. People need to tell the stories of their lives to others. I am acutely aware of this when I travel, and the stranger seated next to me on the bus or plane begins to tell me about his or her past. In a world where we are cut off from the small community where everyone knew our life story, in a society in which people feel alienated from one another, people tend to confide in their hairdresser, the cab driver, or the bartender. Telling an anecdote to someone gives value to your point of view, and indeed, gives value to the way you are living your life.

CHAPTER I

Stories are a lifeline that connect us to our past.

In the process of reflecting about their lives, people often see patterns, recognize how certain of their personality traits developed, and this helps them come to terms with who they are at this stage of their lives. They understand themselves better, and accept why they made certain choices or decisions, how they developed particular attitudes. One man in his seventies told me that he always expected his children to be as hard-working as he was himself. This had been a point of friction when his children were teenagers, as it is in many households. In the process of telling the stories of his life, he suddenly realized that his attitude was shaped by his own upbringing as a Depression child on a farm. In his childhood, there was no time for play, and he carried an abhorrence of idleness with him all his life. By recognizing this influence on his life, he came to terms with his own behavior, and was much more charitable in his judgment of himself and his children.

There is no doubt that reminiscing and telling personal stories has great therapeutic value. Especially as we age, looking back to childhood and young adulthood allows us to integrate those images of our former selves with who we are now. It's a little like superimposing a series of photos of ourselves, from infancy on. We suddenly understand that each photo has contributed to the development of the next, and that the images really are of one person. And particularly in a society which seems to be changing around us so rapidly, where we might find ourselves living far from family or friends who knew us in past years, it's terribly important to keep in touch with these images of our former selves. By making connections between our past and our present, we can look more confidently to the future. Psychologists call it "integration" or "self-acceptance" and believe that it contributes greatly to serenity in old age.

Relating family memories involves a relationship between the teller and the listener. Whether the listener is a son or daughter or grandchild, a hairdresser, a home care nurse, or a friend, the telling creates a human bond, a connection that is very important and meaningful. And that kind of communication is always healing. When we share our memories, whether happy or sad, our philosophies and insights, we celebrate the most human part of ourselves. We give something that is more valuable than any material gift can be because it is the gift of ourselves.

It can sometimes be valuable to share memories which have a strong emotional impact. By expressing long-buried feelings we can exorcise old demons, and perhaps find peace in areas of our lives that previously were difficult to think about. And we recognize that we were able to transcend those times.

Most people are delighted with the chance to record their memories in a way that will be preserved for their grandchildren. They may have told some fragments of stories, or written some down, but a tape recording can put family memories into a chronological framework, and ensure that they won't be lost. While it may be tiring to probe long-forgotten memories, and to respond to questions, it is a very satisfying thing to do. The result is the most precious legacy possible, an oral or visual record of experiences and wisdom for future generations.

There can be entirely unexpected benefits to telling your life story. Sometimes the interview itself becomes the catalyst for closer communication with the teller. In opening oneself up to an interview with someone we care about, there is a rare opportunity to say things that one might not otherwise have said. I once interviewed a man in his eighties, a rather reserved man who rarely expressed his emotions to his four adult children. But in the tape, he addressed the children directly, and, his voice a little choked up, told them how much he loved them. It was easier for him to do it on tape than face to face. The effect on his children when they heard the tape was profound. They understood their father much more clearly, and were more able to express their love verbally with him. In fact, the following Christmas, they got together and made a tape for him, telling him how important he had been in their lives. The original tape

11

recording was important in itself as a record of his remarkably eventful life, but it was also the catalyst for establishing a new and closer relationship with his children. Although he passed away a few years afterwards, the tapes remain as a precious legacy.

What it means to the interviewer

The process of interviewing a relative or friend is as valuable for the interviewer as for the teller. Besides giving us a sense of connectedness and family history, the stories might reveal to us family traits that we have inherited, ancestors with whom we feel a special link, places in the world which now have a particular meaning for us.

It frequently happens that interviewing a parent can reveal things about ourselves as children that delight us, as well as showing something about the values of the teller. There's a story of my husband as a child which my mother-in-law told me, and which I treasure. She was doing the dishes one day, when she looked out of the window. There was her four-year-old son limping towards the house, and crying for all he was worth. As she watched, he suddenly stopped crying, sat down on the sidewalk and all by himself administered the first aid he was coming home for: a kiss on the toe. That taken care of, he scampered back to his playmates. Now why would my mother-in-law select that particular incident and keep it in her memory? When I think of that story now, I realize that one of my husband's strengths is his independence. The trait of thinking independently and relying on one's own resources is highly valued in his family.

While telling stories of our lives has very clear therapeutic value, it is also healing for those in the family who hear the stories. So much of who we are, how we relate to others, and how we approach life in general is formed by attitudes and patterns learned in childhood. By understanding our parents, and what made them the people they became, we can better understand ourselves and our relations with others. When we are able as adults to revisit our childhood through these stories, we sometimes understand more clearly what our parents were going through at a particular time in their lives. A woman in her forties interviewed her father at length, and tells how she gained a new perspective on a period of her own life:

> I have a memory of leaving to go to a birthday party and having a very ragged dress on. And of my mother, on the way to the party, rushing into a clothing store and buying me a fancy dress. My feeling around that was, "You should have thought of that beforehand. Don't you care about me? Don't you love me?" Well, I was looking at some old slides with my dad, and it was the time of that birthday party, and my mother was about seven months pregnant. And she had four young children! And suddenly, I realized that it wasn't that she didn't love me. It was because she was pregnant, and had four children under the age of six, that she didn't have time to think about whether my dress was brand new. She's dead now, so I can't ask her about it. But I could ask my father what was happening around that time. When I asked him why my memories are so sad around that time he said, 'Well, my business wasn't doing well. Mom was about to have another baby.' And suddenly I saw that it wasn't *my* fault. Suddenly I realized that she *did* love me. I'm a mother and I understand. If I had four kids and was pregnant, the last thing I'd be worrying about would be my daughter's dress.

Such insights into our parents' lives can be valuable in other ways as well. Family stories provide a pattern for understanding the experiences of everyday life that can help us as we go through the many stages of living. Although we make our own choices and choose our own paths, those paths can be illuminated by the wisdom—and sometimes folly—of those who have been in similar situations before. Stories go deeper than the intellect. It's not that they help us by

When we share memories and stories we celebrate the most human part of ourselves—we give the gift of ourselves.

prescribing the right way to act, but in recognizing our shared humanity, and the human experience that we have in common, they do help us in our growth and learning.

It's clear that our attitudes and personalities are shaped largely by the environment in which we grew up. Hearing stories about our parents' lives allows us to recognize where some of those traits come from. A writer born in 1942 in England grew up with stories of "making do" during wartime. She tells, "There was a story that was part of the family mythology about my grandmother. Her house had been bombed one night, and my other grandmother who lived quite near, got up in the morning, went over to see if she could do anything, and found my grandmother standing in the middle of the rubble doing the dishes. She had made breakfast with whatever was left, and she was doing the dishes and singing at the top of her voice." The writer realized much later how much her own equanimity in the face of disaster was shaped by the stories of how her family coped during the war.

If we have children ourselves, the family stories we hear give us a sense of dynastic time—a continuum that reaches far back in time and forward in time through our own children. Knowing the family stories that bind the generations together, allows us to pass on to our children the sense that they are part of this ancestral chain.

People who have interviewed their parents invariably find it leads to a deepening of their relationship. One man, who taped an interview with his mother at the seniors' home where she lived, was able to really understand with all his heart that his mother was not always a wheelchair-bound, slightly forgetful, and crotchety elderly woman. He remembered that she had led an active and vibrant life. The mother, on the other hand, in remembering her childhood and young adulthood, was able to be more tolerant of her rambunctious grandchildren, and also of her son, who she felt came to see her *far* too infrequently.

Merely taking the time necessary to talk with a parent, to look

him or her directly in the eyes, and ask questions about the past conveys love and interest. And the parent is able to express emotions more openly than in everyday conversation. A woman who did a videotaped interview with her father told me, "We tend to fight a lot, my father and I, but since the time we did the interview we seem to be able to bridge that gap. A few days ago when I was visiting my parents, we started to argue. I just kind of reached out—this is something that would never have happened before—and said, 'Shall we have a truce?' And he stood up, came around the table, and gave me a big hug. And that happens now; we can sort of let things go. And it seems to come from around the time that we did the interview."

When you propose to tape the telling of a family history, you are saying in effect, "I value this enough that I want to make the time to do it and to record it so that I can keep it forever." And what is implicit in this statement makes both participants cherish the interview.

Why make an audio or video recording?

The benefits of telling family stories for both the teller and the interviewer would exist, whether or not the stories were recorded. But we live in an age when technology can preserve the stories to ensure that they won't be lost or forgotten. It means that not only children but siblings and their children will be enriched by the legacy of a taped interview with a family member.

When children are very young, they tend to take their grandparents for granted. Conversation tends to focus on the present rather than the past. Although they might, if they are lucky, know some isolated stories of their grandparents' youth, it is not generally until they are teenagers that they become interested in their family history. At that point it is sometimes too late to ask questions of their grandparents.

Adolescence is the time when a person is discovering who he or she is. And an understanding of the family's past is an important part of establishing one's sense of identity. It is often during the teen years

Sometimes an interview can be a catalyst that brings the teller and interviewer closer together.

that adopted children tend to wonder about their natural parents, and for any child, it's a period of reflection, analysis, questioning. Teenagers want to know where their roots are. If they know their family's past, if they have a sense of its uniqueness and special qualities, they can understand themselves better. And a taped interview with a grandparent will be extraordinarily precious to a teenager who is asking these kinds of questions.

As well as giving a child a sense of pride and connectedness, the tape recording can give an understanding of history that is more vivid and personal that anything read in a book. Society has changed so incredibly rapidly in the twentieth century that it is almost impossible for children to imagine the daily lives that their grandparents lived many years ago. When a 75-year-old grandparent remembers his or her own grandparent, a child has a direct, intimate, and intensely personal link with someone who lived a century and a half ago. One can metaphorically hold hands across 150 years.

In addition, many families have come to North America in the last 50 years from other countries, and their children have little understanding of the circumstances and culture in the country of their heritage. One man recalled for his daughter the small Italian town from where his parents emigrated before he was born. The daughter relates, "He had never been to Boccheglero. But to him it was an alive place, it was very real, and he had a picture in his mind of what the village was like. He had stories from every corner of that village—for example, my Italian grandmother having a big pot on her head to go and get water at the fountain, and my grandfather watching her from a distance and deciding that she was the one for him. This grandmother was raised by *her* grandmother at a time when cataracts were very common. So my great-great-grandmother taught my grandmother to do all of the housework, to sew, and to take care of everything with a blindfold on, in case she ever got cataracts. And because of these stories, I really do have a sense of belonging, there's no doubt about that. The stories are inside of *me* now."

The tape recording is a permanent record of the voice of the teller, which conveys far more than the information contained in the words. The inflections, speech patterns, voice quality, warmth, and humor are as unique as a fingerprint, and often bring a person back to memory more strongly and vividly than a photograph. For a grandchild or a great-grandchild, this is a precious legacy indeed.

Why use an interview format?

Many older people plan to write their memoirs or record their stories on tape for their grandchildren "sometime in the future." But it's hard to get around to it, and difficult to know where to start. The tape recorder only gathers dust; the pages of the beautifully bound diary remain blank. I've purposely used the framework of storytelling, with a "teller" and "listener," because for most people the telling of family histories is best done in an interaction between two people. Telling life stories is most fun and rewarding when done in conversation with someone else; talking to a machine hardly qualifies as conversation. Someone to smile at, someone who will prod your memory will make a big difference. This person can be a son or daughter, a grandchild or a friend. The essential thing is that the listener is genuinely interested and curious to find out more.

The interview format is useful for several reasons. First and most obviously, it provides a framework for the stories. A carefully planned interview helps the teller present biographical details, as well as the colors and emotions of his or her life story in a fairly orderly way. When we think about our childhood, for example, we are flooded with memories and impressions. Such fragmentary memories can be shaped into stories when we are asked specific questions in a meaningful sequence.

When accepting the rules of a slightly formalized interview, people are perhaps more careful, more attentive, than they might otherwise be. They step beyond the boundaries of everyday conversation

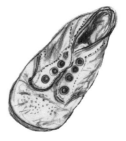

and dig a little deeper for the answers. Similarly, the interview format lets the interviewer ask questions that don't come up in everyday conversation. Sometimes there are things that seem like family secrets; nobody really talks about them. But often it is merely a matter of finding the right time and right space to ask the questions (for more about family secrets see Chapter 8).

Some years ago, I recorded an interview with my own father. After talking for several hours, we came to the war years, a period in my father's life about which I knew very little. I had always assumed him to be reluctant to talk about these years, and was surprised at his openness, and the wealth of stories told with humor and colorful detail which I had never heard. There was not a trace of that reluctance to talk which I had ascribed to him, and so I asked him why on earth I had never heard these stories before. The answer was simple: "You never asked."

A recorded interview can allow metaphorical hand-holding across hundreds of years.

In the role of interviewer, you can remove yourself from your customary relationship with your parent, and ask questions you have always wanted to ask, but perhaps never dared. I've spoken with many adults who feel oddly shy when talking with their parents about matters that touch an emotional nerve. An interview puts both participants on an equal footing, and takes away some of the undercurrents of a parent-child relationship. It is tremendously rewarding and releasing to be able to ask those questions, and equally so for the parent to finally be able to answer them. It is truly a gift that we can give each other.

When people are reluctant to be interviewed

You might find that you are convinced of the importance of interviewing your mother, and approach her enthusiastically, only to be met with a singular lack of enthusiasm on her part. One of the reasons for this might be quite unconscious. The prospect of telling stories of our lives brings us face to face with our own mortality,

something we may not like thinking about. However, it also happens that accepting our mortality can become the catalyst for doing an interview. One woman told me it was only when her father got sick that she realized how important it was for her to do a taped interview with him. And her father welcomed the opportunity of finally telling all his stories in a form that would be permanent and passed on to his family. In fact, he joked about it when she first approached him, saying, "Oh, you want to get this done before I have a stroke!" But there was a lot of truth in this which they both recognized.

Someone recently asked me how she could persuade her father to speak about his experiences as a European Jew during the Holocaust. Whenever she had brought up the subject, he would say that he had no interest in reliving a painful past. There are no easy answers to her question. People deal differently with unpleasant memories of incidents that have scarred them emotionally, whether they are about child abuse, an unhappy marriage, or the loss of loved ones. Some feel that it's better to put the past behind them; others find that talking about it strengthens them and teaches others. And some who found it difficult to speak of these memories earlier may later on choose to do so. I've found that occasionally a grandchild can break down these barriers when an adult child could not. Of course, everyone has the right to privacy and sometimes there will be areas where you have to respect that privacy.

Some people may be reluctant to be interviewed because they feel that their lives have not been special or unique. They think that they have nothing of interest to say and no stories worth listening to. One woman demurred, "Oh, I never did anything unusual. I kept busy raising six children in a sod shack on the prairies; there was no electricity or running water. There was nothing particularly interesting about my life. You should talk to my husband; he's had an exciting life in politics." At such times, the interviewer can reassure them that whatever they have to say will be of great interest and value, and that they will only have to respond to questions. If the interviewer is cu-

rious, caring, and a good listener, it will not be difficult for the teller to find many things to talk about.

Every life is unique, worth reflecting upon and telling—not just the lives of the rich and famous. As we age, we all accumulate a treasure chest full of experiences, choices, happiness and sorrow, regret for paths not followed, pride about particular accomplishments, meetings and partings, and memories that are poignant, humorous, sweet, or painful.

Like fairy gold, the wealth of family stories increases the more you give it away. A tape recorded interview between someone who wants to hear the stories and the person who wants to tell them will uncover that gold and ensure its preservation for future generations. The next chapters will help accomplish just that.

CHAPTER 2

Memory: Steel Trap or Sieve?

*The memory is sometimes so retentive, so serviceable,
so obedient—at others, so bewildered and so weak—
and at others again, so tyrannic, so beyond control!—
We are, to be sure, a miracle every way—but our
powers of recollecting and forgetting do seem peculiarly
past finding out.*
　　　　　　　　　　　　　　　　—JANE AUSTEN

Recently, when one of my teenaged sons was sick with the flu, we decided to watch a movie on TV together. It was a musical made 30 years ago, starring one of the pop stars of my own teen years, and I had only a vague recollection of having seen it. As soon as it started, I was flooded with memories. Not only could I recall every word of every song, but I thought about the time when I first saw the film, who my friends were, and particularly what it *felt* like to be a teenager. My son just raised an eyebrow as I hummed along happily with the music. For my part, I was amazed that so much could lie buried in my memory, and be brought back so vividly by the music. That emotional memory made me feel very close to my son at that moment.

Most of us take our memory for granted, without really considering what an exceptional faculty it is. But just think what life would be like if we didn't have the capacity to remember our past! Memory allows us to relive all the things we've done in our lives, the people we've met, the places we've visited, the books we've read, the music we've heard, the flowers we've smelled. And all those experiences together form the unique person we are at any point in our lives.

A brief history of memory

Before the age of printing, memory was highly valued because all knowledge had to be carried orally through time and space. The Greeks recognized memory's importance by celebrating Mnemosyne, the Greek goddess of memory—a wife of Zeus and the mother of the nine Muses. The first teachers, poets, historians, and religious leaders had to rely not on books, but on the power of their memories and the spoken word to convey their message to others. In ancient Greece and Rome, memory systems were used to enable people to speak for hours without notes. And throughout history, there have been records of truly amazing feats of memory. For example, the teacher Seneca, who lived from 55 BC to 37 AD, asked each student in a class of 200 to recite a line of poetry, and then he recited them back—in reverse order. In the fifteenth century, Peter of Ravenna was said to be able to repeat verbatim 200 speeches of Cicero and 20,000 points of law.

In schools of rhetoric, people were taught how to remember, using a mnemonic system based on visual memory. Because it was thought that people remembered best by using visual cues to associate with words or ideas, they were taught to visualize a particular location or structure that they knew well. Then, as they "walked through" their mental image, they would associate each landmark with a particular point they wanted to make, enabling them to speak for hours at a time without notes.

It was through the power of human memory and the language of storytelling that the thought, wisdom, and mythology of past generations survived through the centuries. The storytellers were not only the trained bards, the itinerant troubadours, the Irish shannachies, but also the ordinary people who would gather around the kitchen fire to tell and listen to stories. A contemporary storyteller paints a vivid picture:

> He would arrive in the late afternoon at an Irish farm, and the children would come running up to greet him and pull him in. And he would have a seat by the fire and have supper, and everybody would go off to do their chores. And then, one by one, they would drift in, and they would arrange themselves around the kitchen fire in order of importance. The farmer himself, the master of the house, his wife, and his children, close relatives, close friends. And then back at the very edge, away from the fire, out in the cold, and farthest from the voice would be poor dependents, the hired man and the people who were less worthy. And there they would sit all evening while the storyteller told his stories, and he had quite a wide variety of tales, some for the small children, some for the older children. The little children would go to sleep when they were tired, and they would just sleep there where they were or on their mothers' laps. And the older stories would then come on. They were mostly hero stories, fairy tales, and stories of the countryside and of the old days. And they would keep his mug filled all evening long. And then late at night, they would all go off to bed because they had early morning chores.

Storytelling as a highly valued art came close to dying out, although it is being revived once more by people who recognize the unique human interaction created by storytelling. But the kind of memory that was crucial to Roman senators was rendered obsolete by the invention of printing. Unless we are actors or actresses, we really have no need to memorize long speeches or poems. Today we

use not only books but computers to do our remembering for us. Very few people make use of the amazing powers that the human brain possesses to remember facts and figures. Memory systems are used as party tricks rather than for serious learning. Why remember a phone number if you can look it up? Why remember what you wanted to buy at the grocery store if you can make a list?

We know now that there are different kinds of memory: the memory for things on a shopping list is very different from the memory of the first day you went to school, or the memory of the smell of a canvas tent you camped in when you were a child, or the memory of how to play hopscotch. It is a challenge for psychologists to come to any conclusions about how something as complex and multifaceted as our memory actually functions. Despite the remarkable scientific advances of recent times, we are far from having achieved a complete understanding.

Do you know when we stopped telling stories in our family? When we bought a dishwasher.

—JW

Memory and the senses

The senses play a crucial role in memory, and the sense of smell has perhaps the strongest relation to memory. A whiff of perfume can evoke your mother, her top drawer, and all your feelings surrounding her. The smell of fresh-cut hay can remind you of summers spent working on a farm and your first summer romance. Walking by the seashore, you might breathe the salty sea air and remember the year you graduated from high school and hitchhiked through Portugal, sleeping on the beaches. The entire context returns—not just one piece of information.

These memories come unbidden, and evoke an entire emotional landscape. My mother once told me that she went for a job interview and came out with an uneasy feeling about it. There was nothing she could put her finger on, nothing particularly unpleasant about the job or the people with whom she spoke. It was only much later that she realized the office was next door to a brewery. The smell of the

brewery must have touched off uncomfortable memories of her elementary school, which was also next door to a brewery. Although her school days had been 40 years previously, the unpleasant feelings came back in a rush with that particular odor.

At university I belonged to a club of outdoor enthusiasts. Every spring, immediately following the last exam, we would head into the mountains on our touring skis, and camp for a week or so in one of the most ruggedly beautiful areas of British Columbia. One of the features of these strenuous trips was the incredibly hot sun, which reflected off the snow and would burn any parts of our faces or arms not protected by the most powerful sun block we could find. To this day, the smell of this cream conjures up the exhilaration and sense of camaraderie and romance of those mountaineering trips.

Why are smells so evocative? A smell is not something you can touch or see; it permeates a whole scene, filling in the cracks in a specific environment. Thus, when you encounter that same smell later, the entire scene comes back. With one whiff, you remember the whole world as you first experienced it.

Almost as evocative as the sense of smell is the sense of hearing. Sounds can bring back the flavor and mood of past experiences in a very strong way. They bring back whole chunks of memory, not just the words of a particular song. Lullabies, for example, bring back the feeling of being rocked and sung to by someone who loved you as a small child. People who have lived through the Second World War are transported back to that time when they hear songs sung by Vera Lynn. And they will hear the songs with a mixture of sadness, patriotism, nostalgia, or regret, depending on their particular war-time experiences. A piece of music that was played at your wedding will always have strong associations for you. When you hear songs from your teen years (which you probably remember by heart), they are likely to bring back feelings you had as a teenager. You might remember feeling misunderstood by your parents, you might remember the time you broke up with your first boyfriend, you might

25

remember the time you first danced with the girl you'd been trying to get to know all year.

A singer once told me about performing in front of a group of seniors. When she sang "You Are My Sunshine," she noticed a woman in the front row who was not singing along, but who was visibly moved by the song. Afterwards this woman told her, "That was the song my grandfather sang for me, and only for me. He never sang it for my brother or sister. It was our song, and when you started singing it, my grandfather was beside me. He's been dead for many years, but I saw his face."

Other sounds as well as songs evoke memories. A woman who grew up in Germany remembers the many church bells she could hear all ringing together. And together with the bell sounds, she remembers the bird songs. When she now hears these sounds she is flooded with memories from her childhood.

As for the sense of taste: there is a famous passage in Marcel Proust's masterpiece, *Remembrance of Things Past,* in which the hero takes a bite of a cake called a *petite madeleine,* which immediately transports him back to his childhood. For me, the taste of cherry strudel brings to mind summer visits with my grandparents in New York City. Every time we visited, my grandmother would buy cherry strudel at a nearby bakery, because she knew that my brother and I loved it. Mom's apple pie, the sweetness of candy floss, even the unforgettable flavor of cod liver oil remind us that taste, particularly that of food eaten in childhood, is closely linked with memory.

Of course, memory is also associated with what we see at a given moment in our physical surroundings. When we revisit a town we lived in years before, people and places come to mind that we haven't thought about for some time. The police know that if they take a witness back to the scene of the crime, that person is better able to reconstruct the events there than at the police station.

Despite the poetic descriptions in our literature of the mysterious power of memory, it is only in the last hundred years that scientists

Take a tape recorder along when you visit family members in your native country.

26

have been studying human memory. And most of these studies have involved factual memory, involving words. If someone is asked to remember a series of words, it will be easy to measure if he or she has remembered correctly. But how do you measure a memory about what the sausages at your boarding school tasted like? How do you explain how a taste of the cake conjured up an entire world for the hero of Proust's novel?

Selective memories

Although psychologists certainly don't have all the answers, they have drawn some interesting conclusions. The first point is that memory is strongly associated with our emotions. If you learn something or experience something in a particular emotional state, for example, you can recall it most easily when you are in a similar emotional state. If you are feeling happy and relaxed, you are more likely to recall happy memories than sad ones. Memories of periods of loneliness or depression come to the surface when you are feeling a little blue.

The connection between memory and emotion explains why childhood and adolescent memories can be so strong. Emotions are generally more volatile during our early years than later on. People, events, and places have a stronger impact than they do in later life, and are encoded in memory with more elaborate cues for later recall. Also, remembered childhood events are likely to be ones that were out of the ordinary: the first day of school, the day Mother brought a newborn brother home from the hospital, the day you fell off the roof and broke your arm. As life becomes more routine, you are less likely to "lay down" a rich and vivid memory than when you were younger and more impressionable.

There are three steps to the memory process: laying down the impression, storing it, and retrieving it at a later time. Some people have likened the human brain to a computer. But scientist David Suzuki believes this to be a misleading analogy, and asserts that the human brain is built on a totally different plan. He says, "First of all, the computer is based strictly on electrical impulses that travel from one junction to the next. Our brains are made out of *meat,* and there are major chemical and hormonal effects. The brain sits in a body, and anybody who has ever fallen madly in love knows that the body affects the way your brain works. I'm convinced that every adolescent who falls in love loses 50 I.Q. points! There's a mind/body interaction that you don't get in a computer,—a very significant difference. And there is a very definite feedback with memory—that is, your particular experiences shape the very way you perceive things. The computer gets its information in one way, in bits and bytes. But the fact is that even though the impulses come into our eyes or our ears in exactly the same way, our ability to receive them is shaped by our previous experiences. Our memory affects our current reality. Computers don't do that at all."

One of the fascinating aspects of memory is why certain things are selectively remembered and others forgotten. When you go to a reunion of your high school class, you will be amazed at the recollections which you thought were gone forever, but are evoked by being with your old classmates, looking through old high school annuals, hearing the music that was popular at the time. But you are just as likely to hear stories about high school pranks which you really have completely forgotten and which others remember clearly.

It would be terrible if we remembered everything that ever happened to us precisely as it occurred. Incidents that are embarrassing beyond belief mercifully fade with time. Difficulties that leave us weeping with frustration become less acute as we look back over the years. Painful periods in our lives, from the breakup of young romances to emotionally difficult periods in our middle and later years, do not absorb us constantly, although the memory of the feelings we experienced can be recalled. Sometimes we have no recollection of an event at all; sometimes it is altered in our memories. This ability to forget is probably essential to our sanity.

We develop a perspective, perhaps even a sense of humor about some difficult periods in our lives. One woman in her eighties was talking about her pioneering life on a homestead, the struggles and the hardships, the crop that failed the first year, the horses that sank up to their bellies in the mud. She was able to laugh about it all as she recounted her stories, but at the time it surely was no laughing matter.

It is clear that our memories aren't like tape recorders on which everything we ever did can be played back. We don't simply record things passively, and we are selective in what we remember. We interpret events, modify them, associate them in new ways in the light of subsequent experience, and selectively forget some of them. It is not uncommon that if several people were in the same place at the same time, each will later remember that moment quite differently, because each has *experienced* it in a unique way.

Often our memory of an event is quite different from the original. Lawyers or police questioning an eyewitness to a crime have to be scrupulously careful not to ask leading questions, because it is quite possible to make someone believe that he remembers something that did not, in fact, happen. If a witness had seen a car leaving the scene of a crime, and the police knew they were looking for a red Volvo, they would not ask, "Was it a red Volvo?", because the witness would likely answer in the affirmative, mistrusting his own memory. Instead, the police would simply ask the witness to describe the car.

We sometimes speak of having a "good memory" or a "bad memory," as if it were one faculty that either works well or doesn't. But how do we explain the fact that we can have a good memory for particular kinds of things, and not for others? Current thinking is that memory is tied to areas of knowledge, expertise, and interest. So, for example, a chess master has an incredible memory for chess moves and board positions, whereas a beginner at chess has trouble remembering the moves. A birdwatcher can remember the names of hundreds of birds. A man who was a pilot when he was young will remember details of the planes he flew, while a passenger in those planes would not. An architect will remember the buildings in a city

Give yourself the luxury of some tranquil time to think about your family stories.

29

she visits for the first time, while the average tourist probably will not. Having a good memory in one area of expertise does not necessarily mean that you will have a good memory in another. There are wide differences among people in terms of what sorts of things they are able to remember and perhaps in what they *want* to remember.

We know now that memory is not one single faculty, but a set of mental skills. Recent research seems to indicate that we have several physiologically distinct memory systems in our brains, and these control our memory for facts, personal experiences, and physical and mental skills.

Why do we forget?

Just as we don't yet know precisely how our memories work, there is as yet no perfect explanation for forgetting. Aside from repressed, emotionally stressful events, for the most part we forget things that aren't of great importance to remember. Forgetting is as useful as remembering, because our minds would be unbearably cluttered if we couldn't get rid of unnecessary information.

One theory of forgetting has to do with interference. For example, we start to make a phone call, something else interferes, we get distracted, and we forget the number we wanted to dial. Or we start to learn Spanish, and the French vocabulary we learned in school gets in the way. But it is thought to be more likely that we forget things because we haven't paid close enough attention to them, we don't attach enough meaning to them, and we haven't processed them deeply in our minds.

We also don't know for certain why we forget memories of personal experiences. Is our memory like a huge warehouse, with everything hidden there, where we just have to find it? Or is it possible for memory to actually decay and break down? There is certainly a lot of evidence to suggest that we can be made to remember much more than is immediately accessible. We know that hypnosis or certain meaningful cues will bring back long-buried memories. But current neuropsychological experiments seem to indicate that the memory connections between neurons in the brain can actually decay through disuse. Certainly, if you experience something that doesn't have a great emotional impact on you, and you don't think about it afterwards, it is unlikely that you will remember it years later, no matter how hard you concentrate. So forgetting is probably a combination of both theories.

Recreating memory

There is a sort of grey area in our understanding of what we do to our memories; we change them, select them, sometimes erase them altogether. For example, many adults remember only the happy times they had when they were teenagers, without recalling the pain and confusion. The baby-boomers, now approaching middle age, are being targeted by an entire nostalgia industry that wants to capitalize on their fond memories of the 1960s.

Memories are more malleable, more changeable than we realize. When my parents talk about their wedding, there is a standing joke between them about who bought the wedding flowers (a 75¢ bunch of sweet peas); my mother "remembers" that she did, my father "remembers" that he did. Who is right? Sometimes what we "remember" is not something that happened at all, but something we were told about. Sometimes we restructure or even reconstruct our memories according to what we've heard or read.

A woman told me about an incident in her youth in which she and her father had dinner with a famous writer of the time. She was an aspiring poet, and was greatly impressed when the writer scribbled some lines on a paper napkin. Later, when she was writing a book for children, she wanted to make the point that a good writer is never without a pencil and paper. She retold the story of the meeting, altering it slightly. In her book, she said that this writer got an idea, and

Hearing family stories gives one a sense of connection, identity, and belonging. Telling them gives shape and meaning to the life of the teller.

wanted to write it down. Not having paper with him, he wrote on the tablecloth, and then paid for the tablecloth when he left. That part of the story was totally made up. Years later, she was talking with her father about the incident, and he absolutely insisted that he had paid for the tablecloth. Nothing she could say could convince him that it hadn't happened at all; it had become a real memory to him.

How the present influences memories of the past

Psychiatrists have pointed out that one's current emotional state has a great effect on one's childhood memories. In effect, the emotion cues a memory that was registered in a similar context. For example, if you are at a playground, and observe a child who is being teased, you are likely to involuntarily remember situations in which you were teased as a child. If you are depressed, and you think about your past, you will remember other times you felt the same way; it will be harder to think about happy times.

Researchers have tracked down people who had been emotionally troubled children. Those who were currently well-adjusted had fewer memories of the turmoil and unhappiness of their childhood than those who were still troubled. We tend to forget those aspects of our lives that no longer fit with our current image of ourselves.

The present can influence memory of the past in other ways. If you are ill, you might remember when your father had pneumonia and couldn't work for a month. As an adult, you might interpret this differently, understanding it from his point of view rather than from a child's more selfish point of view.

Memory changes as we age

Many people fear growing older, because they are certain that their memories will inevitably deteriorate, that their mental functioning will decline. But much of this fear is groundless. Although some loss of memory does occur in certain areas as we get older, it is not nearly as drastic as is commonly thought. And in other areas, there is no loss at all. What probably does in fact make our memories worse is the very *fear* that we will lose our memories; our attitudes and expectations play a large part in the process.

What does seem to happen is that we remember certain parts of our lives much more clearly than others. But this is quite normal; it has nothing to do with a deteriorating memory. The periods of childhood and young adulthood stand out because those are the periods that define us, when we are establishing who we are and our relationship with the world. As we move into our forties and fifties, life is perhaps a little more routine, more stable and therefore less memorable. When we are in our seventies, it's no wonder that we remember things that happened 50 years ago more vividly than things that happened more recently. The implication is not that we *can't* remember things as we get older, but that we have to pay a little more attention to the things we want to remember. For example, when we meet someone for the first time, it's important to very consciously register that person's face and name in our mind. More than 200 years ago, Samuel Johnson said, "Memory is the art of paying attention." It appears that he was absolutely right!

It is also easier to remember something if it has a connection with something we already know and we can attach the new information to an already existing framework. For example, if we are skilled at using computers, it is fairly easy to remember new information about computers. But if the world of computers is altogether foreign to us, we may have difficulty in remembering the most elementary facts about them.

How do we explain the fact that events and people that we remembered clearly when we were younger, are sometimes more difficult to bring to memory as we get older? Perhaps we meet an old friend on the street and are embarrassed because we can't remember the person's name. Perhaps we can't remember exactly where we left

If storytelling doesn't happen naturally in a family, you can create the occasion for it by setting up a simple interview.

33

our car keys. Here the problem is with the retrieval of the information. And again, it's a matter of allowing oneself a little more time, perhaps, to retrieve those memories. Nothing has broken down irreparably, but the process of laying down memories and recovering them is less efficient and slower than it was many years ago.

What seems to happen as we get older is that we remember facts quite well: dates of the world wars, the names of important politicians, the authors of favorite books. And we also remember things that happened in our lives many years ago. But occasionally we have more difficulty remembering things that happened in the recent past: when we last talked with a friend, what we had for dinner two nights ago.

It's important, however, not to blame all memory lapses on aging. Younger people too can "go blank" trying to recollect someone's name when they meet that person unexpectedly. Young people, too, forget where they put their car keys. That's quite normal. The fact is, your very anxiety about memory loss can cause a deterioration in your memory. So can depression, stress, illness, a lack of sleep, certain medications, poor nutrition, a lack of physical exercise, and a host of other factors. The efficient functioning of your mind can't be separated from the overall condition of your body and spirit.

If we are in generally good health, and keep mentally active, there is no reason to fear severe memory loss as we grow older. While memory is not like a muscle that can be improved with greater use, it can function more efficiently if we concentrate on what we want to remember, and as much as possible put ourselves back into similar conditions to those of the event we'd like to recall. We might have to make more lists than we did before, more notes and reminders. Psychologists believe that by taking these precautions and by remaining intellectually active as we grow older, we can count on our memories working well for our entire lives.

Remember the Time: Preparations for the Interviewer

Families everywhere have their stories, many of them entertaining, all of them meaningful, pertinent and binding.
—ELIZABETH STONE

Choosing a time

Your role as interviewer starts long before you set up the tape recorder and ask your first question. Once you've broached the topic of doing an interview with a parent, relative, or friend, don't leap into it right away. You both need time to think about it for a few days at least. And, as the interviewer, you might want to do some advance research.

If you live in the same community as the person you want to interview, establish a time a week or so in the future. You don't want to give your teller enough time to get cold feet! Think carefully about the time of day that you plan to do the interview. If you work during the day, the evening may be most convenient for you. But it may not be a time of day when an older person is at his or her best. Some people in their seventies are up, active, and ready to take on the world by 7:00 in the morning. By the time dinner is over, they are ready to wind down. Of course, this has probably been a life-long pattern. Other people are much slower getting out of bed in the morning, and find that early afternoon is a good time to plan a stimulating activity. Both interviewing and being interviewed are very demanding of mental and physical energy, so plan for a time when you both are at your peak.

Whatever the time of day that you agree on, try to ensure that you won't be interrupted. As much as possible, you want a few hours in which you can both concentrate wholly on the interview. Avoid a day when you know you will be pressed for time or have other things on your mind. It's best to be as flexible as possible, letting the interview follow a natural course without having to cut it short unnecessarily. There's nothing more frustrating than having to turn the tape recorder off when the interview is still going strong because you have to take your son to his guitar lesson!

These days it's more than likely that you have to travel to see your parents or grandparents. Especially if you see them only on rare occasions, you might use the opportunity to record an interview. Of course it's possible to wait to broach the subject until you get there. But you might write or phone ahead of time to tell them that you want to bring a tape recorder along for an interview. And if, quite understandably, they become a little nervous at the prospect, you can put their minds at ease by telling them simply that you want to ask some questions about their childhood, their adolescence, how they met each other, what their lives have been like. Give them some specific things to think about before you arrive. If your father worked on the railroads, ask him to think about some stories of the early days of railroads, some of the people he knew, what the trains were like, how things have changed. If your mother was a teacher, ask her to look through her souvenirs of those days and to remember her first teaching job, some of the children in her classes, what she most enjoyed about teaching. It doesn't take much to stimulate people's memories about the past!

Where to do the interview

If at all possible, come to the home of the person whom you are going to interview. An older person will be much more at ease in familiar surroundings, with a better sense of control over the situation. Another practical reason for doing the interview in the teller's own home is that his or her memory will be helped along by the familiar furniture, pictures, and objects in their own home. It is more difficult for an older person to remember their stories without cues, and the home environment will provide many for exploring the past.

The value of background information

Before you begin to think about the questions that you want to ask, review everything you know about the teller's life. You might think that this would make the interview less spontaneous because you will already know the answers to some of the questions you ask. But in fact, the more you are aware of the outline of the person's life, the more interesting the questions you can ask. And the teller will probe his or her memory for stories and anecdotes that you haven't heard yet. It's like building a house; if you have the structure of the house in mind when you start, you will proceed with confidence and be able to spend some time thinking about the color and detail that make the house unique. If you don't really have any idea of what the house will look like, then all your energy has to go into just making sure that it will stand up!

As a class project, a high school student had to interview an older person. She chose to interview a fascinating woman in her eighties who lived on an island where the student and her family spent their summers. She simply planned to take her tape recorder, set it up, and start asking questions. But it turned out that she knew very little about the woman's life. Had she always lived on the island? If not, when did she move there? Had she been married? Had she had a ca-

Family stories are not only oral history, but also healing.

37

reer? By talking to some of the woman's friends ahead of time, she was able to put together an outline of the woman's life, and so could go beyond asking only very elementary and superficial questions during the interview.

Doing simple background research

You can do research in a variety of ways. First, make some notes about what you already know about the person you want to interview. Then, to fill in some of the blanks, spend some time talking to people who are close to that person. Even if you are interviewing your own mother, there will be things about her life that perhaps you thought you knew, but about which you are in fact uncertain. Talk to an aunt or uncle, or talk to one of your own siblings to see if they know about a particular period in your mother's life. Ask them about specific stories they have about your mother. Ask them if your mother has areas of particular sensitivity. Maybe there's an area that would upset your mother, about which you have to be careful. Ask an aunt or uncle what your mother was like as a little girl; it will help you to frame some wonderful questions. In talking to them, you will inevitably get a new perspective on your mother, and think of more things you want to ask. (You may want to record these conversations on a little dictating machine, and listen to the tape later, at your leisure, as it's hard to listen and take notes at the same time.)

Think also about stories you remember her telling. Perhaps you remember her telling you that she loved a particular doll when she was little. Make a note to ask her about it: on what occasion she got it, what it looked like, why it was so special. Perhaps you have a vague memory of her telling you about a train trip across the country with a girlfriend when she was 18. Again, make a note to ask her more about it.

There is another kind of research with great benefits to you as an interviewer. If you are of a different generation than the person you are interviewing, try to find out as much as possible about the period in which that person grew up. It's worth a trip to the library to flip through some history books and refresh your memory about important national and international events. You will be able to look up newspaper headlines according to the year, and these headlines might give you ideas of questions to ask. You could also look at a copy of *Chronicles of the Twentieth Century* (published by Chronicle Publications, New York) which summarizes the events of the twentieth century by the month.

Find out which music was popular when your father was young and perhaps get a record or tape to play for him. We know that hearing familiar music can bring back rich memories of the past. Look at pictures of the cars that people were driving, the clothes they were wearing, the sports they were playing. Think of all the ways that you can jog his memory to bring stories back.

If you are interviewing a family member, look through old photo albums for people, places, and occasions that you might want to ask about. That picture of your mother holding you by the hand at the edge of a lake. Wasn't that where you always went during the summer? Make a note to ask your parents questions about summer holidays.

Planning the interview

It's important to make a written list of questions before the interview, even if it is only used as a rough guide. The interview will probably follow a loosely chronological sequence, embellished and filled out by the myriad stories that make up the unique life you are recording. Have a look at the sample questions in Chapter 14, but of course adapt them to the person to whom you will be talking. While you might not ask these precise questions, they will give you a useful framework. And having prepared some questions in advance will give you confidence, as well as inspiring the teller's confidence in you.

Handling your role as the interviewer

You may know a great deal about the person you are interviewing, but remember that your main function will be to ask questions and to listen. While you are drawing out the teller's thoughts and ideas, it is also you who will control the direction and pace of the interview. Remember that if you arrive at the person's home feeling confident and positive, this in turn will give the teller confidence. It will also communicate your sense of excitement and anticipation. If you feel relaxed, you can more easily dispel any nervousness that the older person may feel, and the memories will not be blocked by that person feeling stressed.

By understanding our parents and what made them the people they became, we can better understand ourselves and our relations with others.

Because this is a very special occasion you might want to think about what to wear. While you don't need to dress in a formal way, it's best to avoid the other extreme as well. You will know intuitively what might jar an older person's sensibilities! If you wear something bright and cheerful, that will help set the tone for the conversation. If the interview is to be videotaped, avoid wearing black or white, and mention that to the teller when you make your arrangements. Colors with too great a contrast can adversely affect your appearance on video.

I have found that bringing flowers helps make the statement that this is a happy and special time. You will find your own way of celebrating the moment. Perhaps you could bring some muffins to share, perhaps a particular tea or coffee which you know is a treat, perhaps a single rose to put on the table.

Each interview will be unique. There's no way that you will be able to anticipate everything that will happen when you actually turn on the tape or video recorder and start talking together. There are bound to be some surprises! Although you know the teller well, this will be a very different situation for both of you, and you might find the teller more open, witty, nervous, or reflective than you anticipated. Don't expect the moon, but visualize the encounter as you

would like to see it unfold, and your relationship with the teller as you would like it to develop. Strike a balance between what you want and what's possible in your particular circumstances. If you arrive at the teller's door feeling well prepared and positive, then it will certainly be a successful and memorable occasion.

41

What's So Special About My Life?: Preparations for the Teller

When an elder dies, it is as if an entire library burns down. —AFRICAN SAYING

So you've let yourself be persuaded to do an interview about your life, and now you're getting cold feet! "What have I got to say?" you ask. "My life has been pretty ordinary." Don't believe it! Your life is unique. You have become who you are through a combination of background, upbringing, social and political environment, and those most interesting and unpredictable factors of opportunities, choices, and serendipity. No one else has ever lived a life exactly like yours.

Doing a taped interview will let you relive some of the events of your life, and perhaps reflect on some of the people who have been important to you. You'll find that your journey back in time will lead you easily to other memories that are not quite so close to the surface. What starts out as a series of unrelated memory fragments will soon take on a more meaningful pattern.

42

Memory does sometimes need prodding. And although you can be sure that whoever is planning the interview will be giving a lot of thought to which questions to ask, it will be very valuable to sit down for a quiet hour or so a few days before the interview and think about your life experiences. There are some easy ways you can learn to jog your memory, to help you recall events and people that you perhaps haven't thought about for years.

Jogging your memory

Some of the first questions you will be asked will likely call on your memories or stories of the generations that preceded your own. You've probably heard some stories about your own ancestors, which may seem like mere fragments or anecdotes, but will be extremely precious to your children or grandchildren. Sometimes even one image of a great-grandparent is precious to a young person. All I know about one great-great-grandmother is that she once danced before the Russian Czar—in red shoes! Whatever its basis in fact, this exotic story delights me. She may have been at a formal ball. But I prefer to think of her kicking up her heels in an exuberant and slightly shocking dance in front of a startled Czar. Considering our fairly conventional family, I am delighted that her blood flows through my veins!

Some of these stories may be long buried in the recesses of your mind. It will help you remember if you sketch out a genogram, a family tree with more detail (see Chapter 12), going back as far as possible. Try and remember any stories you may have heard about your grandparents and great-grandparents. Can you think of any details that would make them come alive, any particular features of their personalities, what they looked like, where their names came from? Look back over any photos that you might have, and select some to show the interviewer. Perhaps there's a picture of a young man in a military uniform. Who was he? Isn't he your great uncle who died in World War I? How did that affect your grandmother

I don't really understand my own life until I have storied it and told it to someone else.

—IG

43

and her family? Think about all the ancestors on your family tree, and try to remember as much detail as possible about them.

- Think about your life, starting at the very beginning. What is your first memory? Do you remember the house you lived in as a small child? What did it look like? Did you have your own bedroom? A secret hiding place? When would you go there? Can you think of a story of something that happened when you were hiding there? Imagine yourself as a small child. Try to remember games and toys, the first day of school, swimming in the summertime. Remember that small details, which may seem commonplace to you, will be treasured by your children and grandchildren. Their lives now are very different from your past, though their emotions may be quite similar.

- Close your eyes and think of some of the smells you re-member. What about the smell of holiday baking, or the Christmas tree? What stories do those smells evoke for you? What about the smell of the clover growing in the summer by your house? Did you play there? With whom did you play? Did you have a lot of friends, or were you by yourself much of the time? Do you remember the delicate scent of the violets you picked with your sisters in the springtime? You were careful to bind the bunch with soft wool, so as not to bruise the tender stems, and then you brought them home to your mother. Do you remember barnyard smells? That should bring back a lot of memories!

- Can you recall any sounds? The sounds of horses' hoofs clattering over cobblestones, sounds of the wild geese as they flew overhead in the fall and spring, or sounds of the ice breaking up in the lake, a sure sign that it was time to put away the skates for another season! Can you remember

what the steam train sounded like as it pulled into the station? There you were, suitcases in hand, heading off to school or a first job away from home. Who was there to see you off? How did you feel about leaving home for the first time?

- And try to remember some tastes. The tiny wild strawberries that exploded with sweetness! It took forever to pick a handful, but they were so delicious! The taste of candy apples when your grandfather took you to the summer fair. Think about the fair and if there was a merry-go-round. Do you remember the lemon meringue pie that your aunt would make every time you came to visit? What else do you remember about those visits? What about the taste of the cod liver oil your mother insisted that you take every day? That one's hard to forget!

- Are there any particular textures that bring back memories for you? Can you remember what it felt like to walk barefoot in the sand? What kind of scene does that conjure up for you? When you feel a rough tweed material, do you think of your father? What kind of man was he? Does petting the neighbor's beautiful collie make you think of your own childhood pet? You used to go off into the woods for hours with only the dog for company. And how heartbroken you were when he died of old age. In the winter, do you pick up a handful of snow, shape it into a ball, and remember the rough and tumble snowball fights you used to have, the forts you would build?

- Think of both happy and unhappy emotions, and the memories that arise from them. When have you felt frightened in your life? Perhaps you wandered away from home as a very young child and couldn't find your way back. When you and your friends were walking over a railway bridge one evening and you suddenly heard a train ap-

*The greatest gifts we
can give our children
are roots—and wings.*

proaching? When as a young man in the war, you were faced with the reality of life and death? When your husband was hurt in an accident, and you didn't know whether or not he would survive? Try to recall some happy emotions, like falling in love, or your pride when you became a parent for the first time, or satisfaction at having achieved an important goal. There are happy times that will certainly stand out in your mind, though perhaps not as isolated incidents but as periods in which everything was going well in your life.

- Jog your memory by looking over old photograph albums, letters, newspaper clippings, school annuals, souvenirs from trips, war medals, pressed flowers, mementos—anything that you have kept because of its particular significance to you, or because it represents an important period in your life.

- Think of all the ways that things you take for granted today are different from your everyday life when you were a child, and how much has changed since then. The transition from horse and buggies to space travel, from party lines on telephones to the rapid communication systems we have now, from the wood stove you cooked on, to the most modern electrical kitchen appliances. Just a straightforward description of your everyday life of years ago will be fascinating to your grandchildren.

How stories emerge from your memories

Everyone has a different style of telling anecdotes, depending on their personality and interests. If a couple goes on a vacation, they will likely tell completely different stories about their holiday. One might start at the beginning and proceed chronologically: where they went, where they stayed, what they ate. The other might paint a few vignettes of the area they visited, by describing a particular person they met, a souvenir they bought, the countryside they saw. While some people appear to be natural raconteurs, able to take the slightest incident, and talk about it in a way that can spellbind an audience, everyone can tell their family stories. So, as you consider the interview that you are about to do, spend a little time thinking of the questions you might ask yourself.

While you are reminiscing, stop at the images or emotions that are particularly vivid in your mind. Try to fill them out with the people, places, and feelings that surround the memories. Good stories answer the basic questions of who, when, where, how, and why. So, for example, if you remember a special toy from your childhood, concentrate on what it looked like and how you felt when you got it. It does not need a lot of extraneous details to make it a wonderful story.

Often, giving an incident the shape of a story and telling it to someone makes it more real, more substantial. In a sense, you own the experience by putting it into a story. And that's when you can stand a little back from the original experience, distance yourself, reflect on it, and understand what it meant to you. When you tell about an incident, you instinctively shape it into a story by deciding what details are important. For example, if you are in a car accident, and are telling about it later, you will leave out some details and emphasize others. You will choose elements that are vivid and most essential, leaving out the ones that needlessly clutter the story. This process continues with time as you tell and retell the story several times, until it feels right to you. And that's the form in which you will remember the story later on.

Here's one memory, told by a 75-year-old woman who grew up in central Europe. She conveys a great deal in just a few sentences:

> I remember going looking for mushrooms with my father. He loved doing that. We got up at 3:00 in the morning, just he and

When I was younger I could remember anything, whether it had happened or not.

—Mark Twain

I, and went into the forest to look for mushrooms. He was a heavy-set man with a bit of a paunch, but he liked to walk. And he had a knack for finding mushrooms. He always seemed to know what piece of earth to turn over with his walking stick, and there was no greater pleasure than to find one of the beautiful 'Herrnpilze' or 'Steinpilze.' Now mind you my father didn't like *eating* mushrooms, that's one thing I've never forgotten. He loved to look for them, but the rest of us ate them.

One of the secrets of storytelling is to be confident that what you have to say is worth listening to. If you feel at all apologetic, this will show in how you sit, in your voice, and the way you answer questions. Remember that the person asking those questions proposed this interview because he or she really wants to know about your past!

You will find that the more you dwell on your recollections, the more memories will come to the surface; it is truly amazing how much you can recall if you give yourself the opportunity. Memories will certainly trigger other memories. But it's important to feel relaxed and to allow yourself the luxury of time in which to think about the questions you will be asked. You need to take the time to think about your life, and to contemplate it in the silence of your thoughts. Remember, too, that you alone do not bear total responsibility for this interview; there will be someone who cares for you asking questions, responding to what you say, prodding your memory, helping you to remember. You will find that the energy of the interviewer also brings fresh energy to you. And you will find that together you are able to reconstruct the important features of your past. Know that you are doing something wonderful for yourself, your children, and your grandchildren by telling them the stories of your life.

An internationally known storyteller, in talking about real-life stories, said, "There's something that we can do for each other by telling people how it was. Now, I don't mean to always live in the past either. But there's a melding of past and present through story. I don't know how that magic is accomplished. You can't bottle it like ketchup. It takes human interaction, and I think that's what story-telling is all about. It's not just images and emotions, it's human interaction, and we need more of it."

Props for the interview

If the interview is being videotaped, you might want to collect some things which will help jog your memory and also be interesting to videotape:

- An atlas to show where the family came from originally, how it has dispersed, how its members ended up where they are now.
- A family tree or a genogram, so that you can refer to various members of previous generations and show how they fit into the family.
- Photo albums which will surely spark reminiscences about people, places, and situations of years gone by.
- Some clothing of particular significance, like a wedding veil, a military uniform, a team baseball hat.
- Newspaper clippings or scrapbooks from periods in your past.
- Special jewelry or other mementos with particular meaning for you.
- A musical instrument you might enjoy playing at some point in the interview.

CHAPTER 5

Audiotaping Your Interview

*You don't look back along time but down through it,
like water. Sometimes this comes to the surface,
sometimes that, sometimes nothing. Nothing goes
away.* —MARGARET ATWOOD

One advantage that we have over previous generations is the readily available technology necessary for recording and preserving the stories of our elders. We don't have to be professional broadcast journalists or television camera operators to use the equipment. Still, we do need to make some decisions as to exactly what we are going to use, and to become familiar with it before launching into the interview.

Audio or video?

The first decision to make is whether you want to use a tape recorder or a video camera to record the interview. For most of us, tape recorders are cheaper and more readily available than video cameras. They are also perhaps less intimidating; an older person can get used to a microphone much more easily than to being videotaped by a camera. There is something about the video camera that makes people of *all* ages quite self-conscious. As one man said, "As soon as I see the red light go on, my IQ drops about 50 points!"

There is another advantage to using a tape recorder rather than a video camera. When you speak across a microphone, you can look the teller directly in the eye, establishing a warm and intimate atmosphere for the interview. If you want to videotape the interview, you either have to manage the camera and the questions at the same time (a daunting prospect, as both tasks take tremendous concentration), or have a third person manage the camera during the interview. No matter who the third person is, the atmosphere in the room will be less intimate than if there were just the two of you. The situation might take on the aspect of a performance rather than a quiet conversation.

Another question to consider is whether you want more emphasis on the visual or the aural aspects of the interview. If your interest is in capturing the nuances of the voice and the stories of the teller, then audiotape is actually preferable to videotape. When the teller is recounting memories from his or her youth, listening to the voice allows you to imagine that young person. But if, for example, you are watching someone elderly and frail on a video, it will be more difficult to imagine that person as a child, leaping off rocks into the swimming hole, or driving a horse and wagon to school, than if you just listened to their voice on a tape. Audiotape demands that the stories take shape in the imagination of the person listening to them. Just reflect for a moment on how you listen to a story on the radio, and contrast it to how you listen to a story told on television.

In terms of listening afterwards to an audiotape or watching a videotape, the audiotape is clearly more versatile. You can listen while in a car, while cooking dinner, or even while taking a walk. To watch a videotape, you have to sit in front of a television monitor.

Whichever you decide to use (and the decision should involve the teller as well as the interviewer), be sure to choose equipment with which you are comfortable, and then become familiar with it before you try to record the interview. The day of the interview is no time to start figuring out how it all works!

The tape recording is a permanent record of the voice of the teller, which conveys far more than the information contained in the words. The inflections, speech patterns, voice quality, warmth, and humor are as unique as a fingerprint.

Things you need for audiotape recording

A few years ago, I convinced a friend to record an interview with her mother, a woman in her seventies who had led, and was continuing to lead, a rich and full life. My friend was delighted with the flow of the conversation, learned a great deal, and felt that her relationship with her mother was immeasurably enhanced by the close hours that they had spent together. But one aspect was a bitter disappointment. When she played back the tape, she could barely make out the words. She had used a small tape recorder with a built-in microphone, which she put off to one side of the table, so as not to interfere with the interaction between her mother and herself. The result was a very poor recording.

So, even if it involves a little more effort or even cost at the outset, I urge you strongly to record the interview with great attention to the quality of the recording. Consider what you are recording as a work of art, as well as a piece of family history. It will be far easier to listen to a tape on which the voice has been clearly recorded than one where you have to strain to understand each word. A well-recorded interview will be treasured far more in the years to come than one that was badly recorded. And this is not at all difficult to achieve.

TAPE RECORDERS

There have been extraordinary advances in audio technology in the last fifteen years, particularly in the quality of cassette machines. Many good quality home cassette decks and portable cassette recorders that are on the market now are perfectly adequate for voice recording. Make sure that you have a tape *recorder,* not just a *playback* machine. If you already own a tape recorder, experiment with it by recording your voice, and perhaps involve a member of your family in a trial question and answer session. Then play it back, and listen to how clear the recording is. If you are dissatisfied with the quality, consider renting one from a reputable audio dealer.

There are two particular features that you should look for to ensure a good quality recording:

A microphone input jack The closer the microphone to the source of sound, the better the sound quality will be. It is, therefore, far better to use an external microphone connected by a cord to the tape recorder, than to rely on the small built-in microphone that may be part of your machine. The built-in mike is usually of low quality, and will pick up noises from the machine itself, as well as ambient sound in the room.

Dolby B or C The Dolby noise reduction system is an electronic process which produces a better quality audio signal by reducing background noise and tape hiss. Keep in mind that tapes recorded on Dolby B or C have to be played back through the same type of system on which they were recorded. Some tape recorders have what is called *Dolby HX Pro,* and these present no compatibility problem. Tapes recorded on them can be played back on any deck.

You may find it convenient to use a machine that has these features:

A pause button Aside from the machine's recording capacity, it is also advantageous to use one with a Pause button. During the interview, you may occasionally want to stop the tape for a moment while the teller thinks over a question, or coughs, or just needs a short break. It will draw far less attention if you can put a finger on the Pause button, than if you loudly click off the machine with the Stop button. But don't forget to start the tape rolling again when you are ready. (Some machines have voice activated recording that automatically pauses the tape when the person being recorded stops talking.)

Automatic shut-off You will appreciate a machine that stops automatically at the end of the tape. When you hear the click, you will know immediately that the cassette tape has run out, and it is time to flip the tape over or to insert the next one. Without this, it is easy to become so absorbed in the interview that you lose track of the time, and are unaware that you have reached the end of the tape.

The interview provides a framework for asking questions that perhaps haven't been asked before. It can give shape to a lifetime of memories, impressions, and experiences.

53

Earphones Another useful item is a pair of earphones for monitoring the recording as you go along. You need not get an expensive set, since all you want to do is hear what is being recorded—or not recorded. There is nothing more frustrating than conducting a brilliant interview, only to find afterwards that you have forgotten to push the Record button. Listening through earphones will let you catch that mistake right away!

THE MICROPHONE

Since the microphone is the point at which sound becomes electric energy, a good microphone can make a great deal of difference to the quality of your recording. While you can't tell by looking at them, microphones differ not only in their quality, but in their pick-up patterns.

Unidirectional (cardioid) microphones have to be pointed directly at the speaker's mouth, since they have a rather narrow acoustic focus. They are most useful in a noisy environment, when you want to exclude surrounding sound. If you are using a unidirectional microphone, you have to either mount it on a stand directed at the teller (in which case your questions will be less audible than the teller's answers), or you have to move it back and forth between yourself and the teller. Unless you are very experienced, hand-holding a microphone runs a great risk. The microphone will pick up noise from the cord, as well as from your fingers as they move on the microphone itself. An additional risk is that you find yourself so totally absorbed in what the teller has to say that you forget to position the microphone correctly. Any erratic movements with the microphone will result in irritating changes of volume on the tape.

Bidirectional microphones or omnidirectional microphones are the most suitable for interviews, especially in a quiet setting. They will pick up the sound on both sides, including your questions as well as the teller's answers. If you are sitting at a table at right angles to the teller, you can mount the microphone between you on a small desk stand. Ideally, the microphone should be about ten inches from the

speaker's mouth, certainly not more than two and a half feet. If you are sitting side by side on a sofa, it is more difficult to place the microphone close enough, but you can wedge it upright between some pillows. Either of these methods is preferable to holding the microphone in your hand, since each will eliminate extraneous noise on the tape.

The lapel microphone is a great invention. You can just clip it on to the lapel of your teller's shirt, jacket, or dress, and forget about it. But again, be sure to experiment with it enough beforehand to know exactly how far from the teller's mouth is the best position. Some of these microphones are omnidirectional rather than unidirectional. Though they will pick up more of the surrounding sound—including your voice—they will capture the teller's voice quality more clearly. A person wearing a lapel microphone has to be very careful not to move around too much, because the microphone can pick up the rustling of clothing.

A really sophisticated set-up would be two lapel mikes, one for each of you. Since there is only one microphone input jack on a mono tape recorder, you will have to obtain a Y-cord at your stereo dealer. Each microphone is plugged into one branch of the Y, and the signals are combined into one signal going into the tape recorder.

THE TAPE

When you go shopping for cassette tape you will see that there is a bewildering variety of brands, lengths, and types. Check in your tape recorder's manual to see what type of tape should be used with your particular machine. While the high-priced metal tapes are best for recording music, they are unnecessary for recording voice. The Type II (chromium dioxide) tape is a little more expensive than Type I (normal bias) tape, but I would recommend you spend a bit more, at least for the original recording. When you buy it, read the package to make sure that the tape is at least 1 mil (one thousandth inch) thick. Choose a reputable brand, and look for cassettes that are screwed to-

Although we know that cassettes can be stored for a long time, you might choose to transfer your interview to some new technological format in the future.

gether rather than glued; this makes it far easier to open them up to repair them should it become necessary. You will be using this tape to make copies afterwards, so it's worth spending a few extra dollars to get good quality tape on which to record the interview.

The 60-minute tapes are an ideal length. The longer cassettes (90 minutes or 120 minutes) are made with thinner tape so as to fit into the same size cassette case. Although today's tapes are of far superior quality than they were even a few years ago, tapes less than 1 mil are more susceptible to stretching, breaking, or becoming entangled. Another disadvantage of thin tapes is that they are more likely to cause "print-through." When this happens, the signal from one layer of tape is transferred to the next layer, so that the listener hears an echo of the earlier signal. This may occur when tapes are stored for a long period of time. It can be prevented by "exercising" the tape (running it at high speed forwards and backwards) every six months. As an additional precaution, you might get the cassette dubbed on quarter-inch reel-to-reel tape.

Audio technology is changing rapidly, and the direction those changes will take is still unclear. Digital audio recorders are available, although at an extremely high price. Digital technology is more precise, less susceptible to distortion, and more durable than the analog technology more commonly in use. Recorders using laser technology (optical discs) are being developed for a future consumer market. Just as you might transfer old home movies to video, in the future you might choose to transfer your precious interview from cassette tape to some new technological format, such as digital audiotape (DAT). This will be insurance against loss or damage to the tape if you want its quality to last for your own grandchildren.

Checking out your equipment

Once you have chosen the best equipment that you can beg, borrow, or buy, be sure to familiarize yourself with it enough to understand it.

Considering a life story interview brings us face to face with our mortality, and reminds us that we will not always be around to tell our stories.

Read the instruction manual carefully, because you may find that it has features of which you were unaware. Make sure that you understand everything thoroughly. When the time for the interview arrives, you will want to concentrate wholly on the interview, without having to fiddle around with the equipment. You will certainly put your teller at ease more quickly if you are not awkwardly fumbling with the controls on your tape recorder, or making several false starts. If you have bought or rented a recording machine, ask the salesperson in the store to give you precise instructions on how to use it.

First of all, clean the tape recorder's magnetic heads which make contact with the tape. Oxide particles from the tape can shed on to rubber and metal parts, and even a speck of dust can lower the quality of the recording. Especially if you haven't used the tape recorder for a while, it is worth a few moments to make sure it is in tip-top condition. All you need is a cotton swab which you dip into a head-cleaning solution (from any stereo dealer), and then gently wipe across the heads. This should be done after every ten hours of running the machine. The pinch rollers and capstans that come into contact with the tape should also be cleaned, though not as frequently as the heads. For these, use denatured alcohol, as the head-cleaning solution can cause corrosion of the rubber parts of the tape recorder.

Practice setting up the tape recorder, plugging in the microphone and earphones, popping the cassette tape in, and taking it out. If you use an adaptor, which you plug into a wall outlet, rather than using batteries, you won't have to worry about the batteries running out. If you do plan to use batteries, make sure they are brand new, and that you have some spare ones as well.

Most important, remember to practice using the microphone, to see where you have to hold it for optimal sound. The best way to do this is to ask a friend or family member to go through a mock interview with you. Put on the earphones and listen to what is being recorded. You will very quickly hear how sensitive the microphone is,

What the ear does not hear will not move the heart.

—Joe Neil McNeill

57

A comfortable seating arrangement might be at right angles at the dining room table.

whether a lapel microphone picks up the rustle of clothes or the sound of your own fingers touching the microphone. Fidget a little with the microphone, so that you hear what this will sound like. If you will be using a small microphone stand that can sit on the table, try putting a towel, firm cushion, magazine, or rubber mat underneath to absorb the vibration. Place the microphone a little distance from the recording machine, so as not to pick up the hum of the motor.

Sibilant s's and popping p's will indicate to you how far from the speaker's mouth you have to hold the microphone and at what angle. You will also become sensitive to the background sounds which we normally screen out of our hearing, but which are recorded indiscriminately on the tape. Things like ticking clocks, ringing telephones, buzzing refrigerators, a furnace, or a radio on in the next room can be very annoying. If you have a manual recording level control, adjust the setting so that the recording level peaks in the red zone of the meter.

The best environment for audiotaping

Very likely, the acoustic environment in which you practice using your equipment will be different from the one in which you actually do the interview. But you will also need to think about precisely where you will conduct the interview.

Some years ago, I went to the home of a writer to record an interview for a documentary radio program. He first led me into his living room where his young children were watching television. I told him it was a little noisy, and asked if there wasn't somewhere quieter. So we went into the next room—but you could still hear the television through the walls. It was getting a little embarrassing, because I didn't want to impose on him, and appreciated his giving me an interview in the first place. With a slight air of irritation, he then led the way into the kitchen. Of course, both the refrigerator and the fluorescent lights were buzzing. In addition, the tile floor and painted walls created an extremely echoing acoustic environment. By this time I was certain that the interview would be a disaster, as it was off on the wrong foot altogether. But I screwed up my courage, and for the third time, pointed out the problems with the room. We finally found a quiet little carpeted room at the back of the house where there was no background sound at all. The interview, incidentally, turned out wonderfully.

The moral of this story is that even though you are in someone else's home, you will need to have some input into where to conduct the interview. You might think that the living room will be the best place; that the teller will relax in his or her favorite armchair, while you sit on the sofa, and the two of you just chat. But this isn't really a social visit; this is an interview. You will have to sit close enough to the person to be able to hold a microphone directly under his or her nose.

One possibility is that you sit side by side on a sofa. An even better arrangement is for the two of you to sit at a table, at right angles to each other. In this position, you can easily use a microphone stand. You will be able to look one another directly in the eye, rather than having to turn sideways, as you would on a sofa. As you talk, you can also keep notes on the table beside you, with the tape recorder placed to one side. And, of course, if you sit at a table you can bring a pot of coffee or a jug of lemonade to relax with as you're talking. Where there is a dining room, it is an ideal place to sit comfortably; many dining rooms are carpeted, and have drapes on the windows, providing an excellent acoustic environment. Usually it is some distance away from the sounds of fluorescent lights and air conditioners. Don't hesitate to ask the host or hostess to turn off electric motors that are interfering with the sound.

All this means that it's wise to plan the time of the interview with the sounds in mind. If it's a particularly hot day, and turning off the air conditioning would be uncomfortable, arrange the interview for the cooler evening time. Try to choose a time when you won't be in-

terrupted by ringing telephones, or other people coming home. The fewer distractions the better!

If the person you are interviewing lives in a rural environment, you might consider sitting outside. The sound of birds and animals can be very pleasant and evocative on the tape later on. But it is risky. Sounds of cars or airplanes are not at all pleasant, and even if there is only a light wind, you will hear it rumbling on the tape. Some of the wind sound can be eliminated by using a microphone windscreen—a foam cover sized to fit your particular microphone—which you can get at a stereo dealer. Even an ordinary cotton sock, or, if you're really desperate, a cotton T-shirt over the microphone, will cut out the noise of the wind. If the idea of being outside appeals to you, and if there is absolutely no wind, consider doing part of the interview outdoors and the rest indoors. There's no reason that there can't be some variety in the background sounds of the interview.

If the teller's voice is soft, clip the microphone on the collar; if the teller's voice is loud and booming, clip it lower, by a shirt button or on a pocket.

Other things you will need for audiotaping

Below are a few extra things which you should tuck into a bag to take along with you to the interview:

- A couple of extra cassette tapes, in case the interview runs longer than you anticipate. (It would be a shame to interrupt a stimulating conversation because you underestimated the length of time your teller will want to talk.)
- Spare batteries, if you are using a battery operated tape recorder. The best ones are the rechargeable nickel-cadmium (nicad) batteries. If you are using a condenser microphone that needs its own power supply, remember to bring extra batteries for it, too.
- An extension cord, in case the place you want to set up your tape recorder is too far from the nearest electrical outlet.

- A pen for labeling the tapes as soon as you have recorded them. It is very important to write at least the name of the person, and to number each tape in sequence so that you don't get them out of order. A more careful labeling of the contents of the interview can be done later.
- Some paper for jotting down things that occur to you as you are listening to the teller, which you may want to ask about later on in the interview.

Videotaping Your Interview

He is the happiest man who can trace an unbroken connection between the end of his life and the beginning. —JOHANN WOLFGANG VON GOETHE

If you own or are able to borrow a video camera, it will be very tempting to assume that a visual record of the interview is preferable to a sound recording. Certainly our society is more oriented towards television than radio, and video cameras are a great deal of fun to use.

Bearing in mind the comments made at the beginning of the last chapter about the advantages of audiotaping, there are some reasons for considering a videotape of the interview. Of course, the main reason is that the family will see the teller as he or she is now. You will be able to see the hand gestures, the twinkle in the eyes, the irony expressed by raised eyebrows, the emotion in the face of the teller conveying more than words. But a "talking head" interview in which the picture doesn't change can be boring to watch for more than a few minutes. If you are willing to give some thought to making the tape visually interesting, then do, by all means, consider videotaping the interview.

Although it is technically possible to operate a camera and conduct an interview at the same time, it's not necessarily desirable. The interaction between teller and interviewer is closest when the two people can look directly at one another and concentrate completely on their conversation. If you are simultaneously trying to focus the shot, listen to what the teller is saying, and think of the next question, you probably won't do any of those things well. And the interview will suffer as a result. It might be better to ask someone else to operate the camera—preferably someone known to and trusted by the teller, who won't interfere in the conversation.

A woman who wanted to videotape an interview with her father asked her husband to be her cameraman. He, of course, hadn't grown up hearing his father-in-law's stories, and found them fascinating. He was also very moved by being an observer of the close relationship between father and daughter—one that grew even stronger as they worked on the interview. But he had to be careful not to distract the teller with the technical concerns of setting up and recording the interview.

The technological developments of video camera equipment in the last decade have been nothing short of phenomenal. Not only have prices come down dramatically from the initial models, but their design has been very much simplified. Now even a child can hold and operate a camcorder, which combines both the video camera and the video recorder in one lightweight package. Certainly videos are much easier to make than were the home movies of the past, when films were shot, and then had to be sent away for developing. Only when they came back and were screened could one see if the pictures were badly framed, the lighting too harsh, or the sound poor. Most modern video cameras have built-in screens so that you can play back what you have shot and correct it if necessary. Just as with audio recordings, a little planning and thinking about what you want to achieve will yield a far better result than if you just "point and shoot," as the advertisements say.

Whatever video equipment you choose, take the time to experiment with it well before your interview. Read the instruction manual carefully to make certain that you understand how everything

Memory allows us to relive all the things we've done, the people we've met, the places we've visited, the music we've heard, the flowers we've smelled.

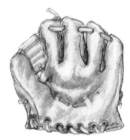

works. Get a tripod that suits the weight of the camera, and practice taping people and objects in your own home. Tapes can be erased and reused, so have fun as you become familiar with all the features of the camera.

Sound

It might seem odd to begin a discussion of video recording with remarks about the sound, but for our purposes, the sound is at least as important as the pictures, if not more so. If you have to strain to hear the words, you will be unlikely to sit and watch a videotape that might last for several hours. If the picture is not terribly dynamic—and while a two-person conversation may be intellectually and emotionally interesting, it will not be visually exciting—a crisp clear soundtrack will help to compensate.

Be aware of ambient sounds such as ticking clocks, traffic, or air conditioners, and try to find as quiet a space as possible for the interview.

The audio portion of video recorders is often sadly neglected. Except for the expensive cameras with hi-fi playback, the sound is of a lower quality than if it were recorded on a cheap cassette recorder.

Most cameras come with a built-in microphone but this will indiscriminately pick up all noises in the room, including room ambience, ticking clocks, or a cough by the camera operator. In fact, a remark made by the person operating the camera will be recorded much more clearly than the more distant voice of the teller. Although you can zoom in to a close-up of the teller's face, the built-in microphone doesn't zoom in along with the picture.

So, just as with audio recorders, an external microphone which can be placed very close to the teller and the interviewer is a great asset. When you connect an external microphone, it automatically disconnects the built-in microphone. Your choices are similar to those outlined in the chapter on audiotaping. You can hand-hold a microphone or set it up on a microphone stand on the table between you. Again, a good choice is a clip-on lapel microphone for both the teller and the interviewer, which connects to the video recorder with a Y-cord.

The many types, degrees of sensitivity, and prices of microphones can be very confusing. Some microphones are better for recording voice than others, and some are incompatible with certain kinds of video equipment. Your best route is to discuss the situation with a person who is knowledgeable about the camera you are using and is aware of what you want to accomplish.

The tape

There are approximately 25 brands of video cassette tape on the market. Although the properties of the tape are established by industry standards, it is wise to stay with well-known brand names. Even if you pay a little more, it will be worth your peace of mind to know that your interview has been recorded on reliable high-grade (HG) tape.

The three most common types of video tapes are the High Eight, Eight Millimeter, and the larger VHS format. VHS is the standard household type and the simplest to use in the long run. If you are planning to rent a video camera for the interview, make sure that you ask for VHS.

If you have made your tape using an Eight Millimeter or High Eight, you will want to tape it over to a VHS tape so you can play it on a standard VCR. Take out the RCA wire connections in the camera, plug one end into the Camera Output outlet and the other end into your VCR Audio In outlet. Press Play on your camcorder and Record on your VCR. If you are uncertain about doing this yourself, ask a technically-minded friend or someone who has done it before to assist. You can also ask a staff member from a video services store for help.

Duplicating your tape after you have transferred it into VHS format it is simply a matter of using two VCRs and making copies. Make sure you make each duplication from the original tape rather than from a copy so the quality is not too far from the master.

It was through the power of human memory and the language of storytelling that thought, wisdom, and mythology of past generations survived through the centuries.

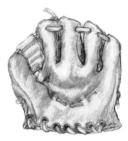

Lighting tips

Unless you have a lot of experience in making videotapes, you probably haven't given much thought to lighting and how to use it to show the teller at his or her best. It doesn't have to be either complicated or costly, and is worth planning a little in advance.

Cameras vary considerably in how much they will adjust for the available light to produce the best possible picture. Some modern video cameras can operate well indoors and if you do the interview during the day, the light might be adequate. Other cameras will require help from extra lighting but even regular lamps can do wonders when fitted with bulbs of stronger wattage.

When you set up the camera at the teller's house, have a critical look at the image on the monitor. Does the light fall evenly on the teller's face, or are there shadows? Can you see the detail on the face? In particular, can you see the teller's eyes clearly or are they dark? So much of a person's character is in the eyes, and it is important to be able to see "the windows of the soul" clearly. If you are not satisfied with the lighting, there are a number of things you can do to improve the picture.

If the teller is sitting directly in front of a window, the camera will expose for the brightest area, and the result will be a dark silhouette against a bright background. Instead, you can seat the teller facing the window, so that the daylight from the window lights the face from the front. Daylight brightens the face and is the softest and most pleasing light.

If it is evening, and you need artificial light, a single 200 watt photo flood light (from a camera store) which clips on to something like a door frame, a bookshelf, or a standing lamp will do the trick. Place the lamp six to ten feet from the teller, at a height of six or seven feet, and slightly off to one side of the camera. If it is placed at too great an angle, it will create heavy shadows on the teller's face.

For outdoor taping, the teller should be in the shade rather than in bright sun, because the light is even and diffused. Experiment a little,

Storytelling as a highly valued art came close to dying out, although it is being revived once more by people who recognize the unique human interaction created by storytelling.

have fun with it, play around with the different effects. And if there are some little shadows on the face, it's not the end of the world!

The camera angle

The more directly the teller looks at the camera, the more intimate the sense created by the interview. The teller will appear to be talking to the viewer of the videotape rather than the interviewer. One way of achieving this is for the camera person to shoot over the interviewer's shoulder.

However, there are also several reasons for shooting the teller from a slight angle. First of all, it's often a little more flattering. And secondly, it is less unnerving to the teller, if he or she is at all uncomfortable with the situation. Avoid shooting the teller in profile, as this is the least flattering position.

In positioning both teller and interviewer, take note of anything in the background that might draw attention away from the interview. Is there a large picture on the wall, or a china collection directly behind the teller that might be distracting to a viewer? If you see anything that could detract from the composition of the picture, you could remove it, change the seating arrangement, or change the camera position slightly to avoid it.

If you watch a lot of television, you will be aware of how the point of view of the camera affects your attitude to what you see. If you view a person from above, it somewhat diminishes him, while viewing from below subtly suggests strength and authority. Since this video is about the life of the teller, the most pleasing effect is achieved by keeping the camera at the eye level of the teller or slightly below.

As with lighting and sound, it will pay great dividends if you have taken time to experiment beforehand to see what works best. If you have familiarized yourself with the equipment, it should take only 15 or 20 minutes to get everything set up and ready to roll.

A tip for learning how to compose shots: Read the comics!

Composing your shots

If you are both the camera operator and the interviewer, you will have to mount the camera on a tripod and simply switch it on. The result will be a static "talking head" interview which is interesting to listen to, but unexciting to watch. However, if you have someone to operate the camera while you ask questions, that person can create a great deal of variety in the shots, and the result will be far more interesting.

The senses play a crucial role in memory, and the sense of smell has perhaps the strongest relation to memory.

When composing each shot, make sure to leave some—but not too much—headroom. This looks more natural than if the top of the head is at the top of the frame. And if the teller moves around a lot, the head always stays within the frame of the picture. Keeping the teller's eyes in the top third of the picture will be the most pleasing arrangement. And if the teller is looking to one side, leave more room on that side. A television producer recommends that the way to learn how to compose shots is to watch a lot of television, and to read a lot of comic strips. (The cartoonist has to position the characters in each box, just as a camera operator must create a pleasing composition of the scene he or she is taping.)

To focus the shot, first point the camera towards the teller, and using the zoom lens, zoom in as far as possible. Focus on the teller's eyes by rotating the focus ring of the lens. Then pull back on the zoom to get the frame that you want. This way, as long as the teller stays in the same position, the picture will always be in sharp focus, no matter what size of picture you set up.

Types of shots

- A wide shot (establishing or geography shot) that establishes the location in which the interview is taking place. This is a good way to start, as it sets the scene. If you are planning to shoot the teller over the shoulder of the interviewer, it might be wise to take this shot from the side to show both people and the room, and then move into position for the rest of the interview.

- A two-person shot, framing the teller and the interviewer.
- A medium shot, framing one person from the chest up.
- A close-up shot, framing the head and top of the shoulders.
- An extreme close-up that frames from the forehead to just under the chin.

For the purposes of this interview, the medium and close-up shots will be most used. Use the extreme close-up for more emotional impact, but, of course, don't overuse it.

Camera movement

The zoom The zoom lens is one that has a continuously variable focal length, that allows you to change the shot so as to make the subject look closer or further away while the tape is rolling. Use this feature with great discretion! Although fun to play with, it becomes tiresome to watch a tape on which the zoom is overused, and the viewer can become quite dizzy! Make sure there is a reason to use the zoom. For example, if you ask an emotionally charged question, it is effective to move in from a medium to a close-up shot. But then hold it there rather than immediately zooming out again. Wait until the moment of tension or drama is over. Instead of simply zooming out again, you might choose to zoom out only slightly, and tilt down to include the hands. The important thing about using the zoom is to think through the entire shot before you start. Where do you want it to start? Where do you want it to end? If you plan it out before beginning, the move can create a very powerful effect.

Panning and tilting You can move the camera either sideways (panning) or up and down (tilting) in order to get from one shot to an-

PRACTICE, PRACTICE, PRACTICE!

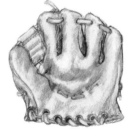

69

When I interviewed my father, my husband operated the camera. He said that being a silent observer gave him an incredible insight into both me and my dad and our relationship.

—AC

other while the tape is rolling. As with the zoom feature, you move the camera only when there is a good reason to do so. If the teller is talking about the set of dishes that she managed to save from a flood, and the dishes are in the same room, then, of course, you will want to show those dishes. You might ask the teller to get up and walk over to the china cabinet, while the camera follows her. Or, as the teller describes his hunting exploits, you might pan from his face to the moose antlers on the wall. As with the zoom, the shot must be visualized *before* you actually embark on it. If you are indecisive in your framing, the flow of the interview will be disrupted, and the viewer's attention will be distracted. But as long as you always have a good reason for doing a pan or a zoom, and are able to execute those moves slowly and smoothly, the variety in shots will be very effective.

Props

In an earlier section, the teller was encouraged to assemble things as objects to discuss, such as photo albums, an atlas, some clothing or jewelry with special significance, or other mementos. Part of the pleasure of videotaping the interview is that these objects can be shown on the tape. Try to have them on a nearby side table, or somewhere within easy reach, so that the teller doesn't have to get up from the chair and walk across the room.

Other things you will need for videotaping

As mentioned in Chapter 5 on making an audiotape, there are a few extra things you should bring along to the interview:

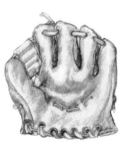

- At least one extra video tape, in case the interview runs longer than you anticipate.
- A tripod that fits the camcorder you are using.
- A 200 watt photo flood light in the event that the inter-

view takes place in the evening or in a dark location (you can rent one from the video services store if you don't have one).

- Spare batteries. Make sure they are the type that fit the camcorder you are using.
- A pen for labeling the tapes as soon as you have recorded them. Write at least the name of the person interviewed and number the tapes in sequence if you use more than one.
- Paper for jotting down notes as you listen to remind you of questions you might want to ask later in the interview.

Shooting a supplemental videotape

Though the making of an audiotape or videotape has been discussed as an either/or proposition, you might consider something a little different. Perhaps the ideal solution is a combination, in which the main part of the interview is recorded on audiotape, with a videotape made afterwards to supplement the interview.

Such a videotape could involve some or all of the following:

- A tour of the house in which the teller lives, guided and commented on by the teller. Knick-knacks and ornaments may hold wonderful stories that were not mentioned in the interview.
- A tour of the garden, especially if the teller has a particular interest in gardening. He or she might even do some weeding for the benefit of the camera.
- Some shots of the teller's daily activities, like making a cup of tea, and starting to drink it, taking a book off the bookshelf and reading it, picking up the newspaper from the front stairs and glancing at the headlines, sitting at the

"Talking head" interviews can be boring, but you can find ways of making the videotape visually interesting.

71

sewing machine, fixing a chair in the workshop, writing at a desk, typewriter, or computer, or running the model train in the basement. In other words, try to reflect the interests and skills of the teller by demonstrating them visually.

- Some interaction between the teller and people close to him or her, such as walking with a friend, having dinner with a spouse, writing a letter to children living in another town, or reading a bedtime story to grandchildren who live nearby.

- Some more active footage of the subject walking down the street, jogging through the woods, riding a bicycle, or playing with the dog.

- Several family members or old friends having a conversation with the teller. This is one circumstance when you as the interviewer might also easily operate the video camera. If you were to ask two sisters to get together and reminisce about their childhood, you would scarcely have to bother asking questions, the stories would fly so quickly. Of course, you would have to be prepared for disagreements or differing interpretations of past events!

If you are a little experimental and have two videotapes, one a "talking head" interview and one a series of scenes, objects, or other people, you may want to combine them. This will require editing or splicing them together. You might also consider adding titles and music to produce a really polished video. For these things you are best advised to take your tapes to a video services store and have them do it. Most places that rent video cameras will be able to edit two tapes together for you.

The only limit to what you can do with audio or videotaping is your own imagination. You may have many more ideas of how to best capture the spirit of the person you are interviewing than I can

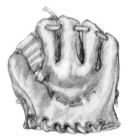

possibly suggest. If you approach the project in a caring way, with an open mind, you will have created a profoundly valuable family memento. If you try something that is artistically pleasing, as well as intellectually and emotionally interesting, you will never be disappointed in the result.

CHAPTER 7

Unearthing Family Treasure: How to Interview

God made man because he loves stories.
—ELIE WIESEL

The day for the interview has arrived, and you have prepared yourself well. You know that the conversation you are about to have will be recorded on tape for posterity, so you are probably looking forward to it with a slight degree of nervous excitement. You know that what happens between the two of you might lead you into new areas of understanding and insight. And what happens in the interview depends a good deal on what you as the listener bring to it. Although you will focus on the anecdotes, experiences, and views of the person being interviewed, you will play a vital part in establishing the mood, drawing out the teller with your questions, and shaping the conversation so that it has a beginning, a middle, and an end.

Establishing the mood

In order for both of you to feel as relaxed and comfortable as possible, you each have to be at ease with the equipment you are using.

While you have had a chance to experiment with the tape recorder, it may be an entirely new experience for an older person to hear him or herself on tape. So take a few minutes to demonstrate how it works; say a few words casually into the microphone, then play back the tape. Have the teller listen to his or her voice through the earphones. This will put your teller at ease, as well as confirming that the equipment is working smoothly. Assure the teller that the tape can be temporarily stopped at any point if he or she wants some time to think about an answer, and offer to answer any questions the teller might have. You might also suggest that you'll stop after an hour or so and take a break.

Sharing a pot of tea while you're doing the interview is a way of keeping the situation warm and relaxed. Although most background sound on the tape can be disconcerting, it is quite nice to hear the friendly clink of tea cups during the conversation.

The tone and degree of intimacy in the interview will depend in large measure on the relationship both people have with each other. If someone is being interviewed by a grandchild, he or she will stress different things, and talk in a different way than if that person were being interviewed by someone of comparable age and experience. Even the stories themselves will be different, and that's only natural. But no matter whether the interviewer is a child, a grandchild, or a friend of the person being interviewed, it is very important to establish at the beginning that the interviewer is attentive, non-judgmental, respectful, and appreciative of the teller's stories and ideas, and is someone to be trusted. The interviewer's aim is not to challenge the teller's memory or point of view, but to provide the opportunity for a full exploration of the person's life.

This sounds straightforward, but family relationships are frequently very complex, and full of friction as well as love. Many of us have mixed feelings towards our parents, and revert to old patterns of behavior in their presence. You may be apprehensive at the thought of trying to interview your parent objectively, without being critical

The connection between memory and emotion explains why childhood and adolescent memories can be so strong.

75

What happens in the interview depends a good deal on what you as the listener bring to it.

on the one hand or avoiding sensitive topics on the other. Yet if you go into the situation with the aim of really discovering who your parent is as a human being, you will find it extremely rewarding.

The interview should be informal and conversational, rather than a cut and dried question and answer session. Unlike normal social conversation where people often listen only long enough to jump in with a comment or anecdote that shifts the focus to themselves, here attention is focused entirely on the teller. So while the tone is conversational and relaxed, the role of the interviewer is very simply to ask questions and listen attentively to the answers.

The art of listening

One of the most important things to learn is the art of concentrated listening. This means more than just sitting quietly and not talking while the other person is talking. It means being wholly focused on that person, giving total attention to what the teller is saying—or not saying. It also means noticing the teller's body language and changes of voice, and being generally aware of the teller's feelings. If you do this, though you as the listener may not be saying anything, you will naturally indicate your involvement and interest with eye contact, and through smiles, nods, frowns, and sympathetic looks in response to what the teller is saying. Don't be afraid of your own emotional responses. I've found myself several times with tears in my eyes because I was so intensely involved with the emotions of the person I was interviewing. It's amazing how eloquent you can be without saying anything. And you'll find that the more deeply you listen, the more positive, responsive, and encouraging you are, and the more genuine sympathy you show, the more forthcoming the teller will be.

As one professional storyteller has said, "It's listening to who the person truly is, more than just the story, because when they're telling you their story, if they really feel an intensity in your listening, they'll tell you who they are. That's when it's really exciting. That's when

76

the person you're listening to gives you the best gift of all: that openness, that honesty—the gift of self."

As the interview progresses, deep listening also involves making mental or written notes about topics to pick up at a later time. This means that although you must appear to be totally relaxed and receptive, your mind is alert and intently processing the information. The teller might allude to an emotion she felt, an incident, or a person; you might not want to interrupt the train of thought at that time, but you can ask about it later. Say, for example, that you are recording your father and entering areas that you'd never discussed together before. You are both treading a bit gingerly. Your father might test the waters with a seemingly off-hand remark about a relationship he had before he met your mother. If you truly want an honest portrait of him, then it's up to you to pick it up and ask about it in a direct yet sensitive way.

Trusting your instincts

As well as listening closely, it helps to trust your intuition and follow hunches. You might, for example, ask your mother a question about her ambitions as a teenager. If she tells you that she always wanted to be a scientist, but was discouraged by her parents and teachers, you will have learned something important about her, and can pursue it further. How did she deal with the opposition to her plans? How has her interest in science affected her in later life? It might give you some insight into why she encouraged your own interests at school. Your objective is to get her to talk freely, not merely to answer your specific questions, so you have to be able to follow the conversation, even if it takes a different tangent than you anticipated. Sometimes, these unexpected digressions lead you into areas that you could not have foreseen and yield the most interesting stories.

A family interview is very different from a media interview; you are not looking for glib answers or prepared stories, but are prodding

At my high school reunion, every conversation I had with people I went to school with 40 years ago gave me a little piece of myself back to me. I really wanted to connect with that person I was in high school.

—FW

77

a little below the surface for memories and emotions that perhaps haven't often been expressed verbally. So don't be afraid of silences or pauses while the teller reflects on your question. If you ask a difficult question, and there is no immediate response, don't apologize for the question, or jump in too soon with a simpler one, because you might miss a truly thoughtful response. Making it clear that you are not in a hurry often gives the teller time to dig a little deeper for an answer. And your accepting silence will be encouraging. Similarly, if the teller has finished answering a question, and you don't have the next question on the tip of your tongue, wait until you've formulated a good one. Don't just jump in with the first thing that comes to your mind in order to fill the silence. You can always use the pause button on your tape recorder while you collect your thoughts.

This is a special experience for both of you. You as the listener/ interviewer can set the mood for the conversation by being warm and relaxed—yet keeping your energy positive. You don't want to be so relaxed that the interview lacks energy! Be prepared, think out your questions carefully, yet at the same time be ready to follow an unforeseen course. Don't interrupt or talk about yourself, but stay focused on what you are hearing. Above all, if you show that you are enjoying yourself, the person whose reminiscences are being recorded will enjoy the process too.

If the interviewer is a child

If the interviewer is a child, this relationship will be very different from the usual relationship of two adults. Children are generally not used to taking charge of a conversation with their elders, much less asking them difficult questions. The teller will have to keep in mind that it is a new role for the child, and that it probably requires a bit of courage for the child to have taken on the role of interviewer. It would be all too easy for the teller to unintentionally intimidate the child. A child's questions should be taken seriously, and answered as fully as possible. Sometimes what children want to know is not at all the same as what adults want to know.

That being said, it is also possible that a relationship that skips a generation can be quite honest and free of the tensions that sometimes trouble parents and their adult children. In all cultures, there is a special quality to the relationship between children and elders.

Asking effective questions

Your role is more than simply recording the stories that the teller wants to recount. You will need to ask questions that will elicit thoughtful rather than glib answers. The more stimulating the questions you ask, the more interesting answers you will receive.

There are some simple guidelines to asking effective questions. If you were to remember only one, it should be this: Wherever possible avoid closed questions that call for a simple "Yes" or "No" answer. Open-ended questions are far more effective. For example, think of how you would respond to the following ways of asking the same question:

- Did you have a happy childhood?
- Tell me some of the happy memories from your childhood. And what about unhappy memories?

Sometimes the more specific a question is, the more personal and eloquent the response will be. Let's say that you're discussing World War II with a war veteran. A very general question would be, "What were some of your war experiences?" And this would probably evoke a fairly general answer. However, you can try to think of more thoughtful questions, such as, "What motivated you to join the air force?" "What did you feel the first time you were in active combat?" "Who were the people in your regiment who were most important to you, and why?" The more carefully you phrase your questions, the

If you're planning a visit with relatives, write ahead and tell them that you want to conduct an interview with them. This will give them time to find photos and diaries, and to reflect a bit before you get there.

more attention the teller will pay to how he or she answers them.

Your approach can affect the pace of the interview; if the teller speaks slowly or is long-winded, you can speed things up by asking short, brisk questions, and the teller will automatically respond more concisely. And you can slow someone down who speaks too rapidly by deliberately drawing out your questions.

You will want to ask quite direct questions when you want factual answers, and more exploratory questions for more thoughtful answers. Sometimes it's effective to follow up a direct question with an exploratory one. For example, if you ask when the teller left school and he answers, "After the tenth grade," you might then ask, "How did you feel about leaving before graduating?" or "Has being without a high school diploma ever been a problem for you?"

Be on the lookout for anecdotes to illustrate the answers to your questions. For example, you can follow up a general question about dating with a more specific question that will allow the teller to reminisce about a particular person or incident. Such stories are often especially memorable and precious to the people who will subsequently hear the tape.

If the teller is a great raconteur, you can follow up some of the stories with a more intimate question about how he felt at the time of the event. In an interview with an 80-year-old ex-bush flyer, he told about his adventures bush-flying in the early days.

Teller: I had a most adventurous trip. It was just one blinkin' adventure after the other. Oh! It was a saga of difficulties all the way through. It was partly the airplane, partly the weather, and equipment. It had no navigation lights, no landing lights, no proper heaters on it—it was wintertime—no radio, of course, and oh, I could write a book on that trip.

Interviewer: What were some of the things that happened?

T: Well, in the first place, the windshield had all glazed over and become yellow. It had been stored in a barn for a couple of years, you see, and

the glass was gone, practically and there was a hole about this big to see through on my side.... The engine was giving us trouble, missing a bit, a single engine, a right engine, about 300 horsepower, I guess. And we had to get to Montreal to get any work done on it. So I was trying to get to Montreal and we ran into weather coming into Quebec City, and fortunately I knew exactly where the airport was, because we had no instruments to find it at all.

I: Did the danger appeal to you? It seems you were taking your life into your hands every time you went up. What was it about the flying that really appealed to you?

As you can see, sometimes your questions won't be proper questions at all, but comments or an echo of what the teller has just said to encourage him or her to keep going. Another example is the following conversation with a woman in her eighties. (You have to imagine her speaking in a Scottish accent!) She was describing the kinds of clothing she and her brothers and sisters wore when they were children.

Teller: I just wore dresses. I was the youngest girl, so Mother never made many things for me. But there was a man used to come around, and he would have a cart. We called him the Bag Man. He'd have all sorts of things in that bag. You could buy dresses or skirts or blouses. My mother said, "Pick something out for Maggie," and I wasn't happy with what he picked out for me. A fleece-lined petticoat, and I didn't want that, and I put it back in his bag.
Interviewer: You didn't like it.
T: I didn't like it, no. It was grey and fleece-lined.
I: What sorts of things did you like?
T: I was very partial to red and blue. And I'm the same yet. Love blue and red. And the dresses then were just plain, very plain, but good. In the school I remember they had a red dress hanging up. And it was all smocked. And it was beautiful. And it was for a prize, this dress. I was always looking at it and looking at it and wondering who was

The more background information you have, the more interesting your questions will be.

going to be the lucky one to get it. And I forget what we had to do to get it, but I won it. So I came home with it and my mother went up to the school and complained. She thought that they thought that I wasn't dressed properly. No, no, they said, it was for a prize, and Maggie won it. I didn't want my mother to take it back. She was quite upset, but when they explained it to her, she was all right.

I: You were allowed to keep it then.

T: Oh yes. I just wore it till it went in ribbons, I think.

Hearing old stories in new ways

Almost everyone has stories that have been told many times before. Particularly if you are a close relative of the teller, you might be hearing about events with which you are already quite familiar. Try to listen with a fresh ear, as if it is the first time. You might find that the intimacy of the interview allows you to gain a new perspective or insight into an old story. You might also find that the story that you *thought* you knew was incomplete; you knew only a part of it. The interview allows you to hear the whole story, and to put it into the context of the teller's life. When a woman in her thirties interviewed her father, she knew about the rural area in which he had lived as a boy, and that he was sent to a private boys' school many miles away from home. But she didn't know how he felt about it. When he told her, in answer to her question, that he had hated coming to the city, and how much he had longed to be back playing with his friends, it gave her fresh insight into him as a child. Although she knew a lot of the facts about his life, she didn't know much about his emotions, and found that doing an interview with him filled out the picture for her.

Dealing with sensitive areas

Of course, if you ask questions that really probe the teller's emotional reactions to events in his or her life, you must be prepared for

Aging does not necessarily mean that one's memory will deteriorate.

honest answers. And you might not like the answers you receive. In one interview, an older person was asked about the plans he had when he was young. The next question was, "Did you follow your dreams?" and the answer very clearly and regretfully was "No." Because the interviewer felt unable to respond or to take the conversation further in that direction, he jumped in too quickly with a question that led the teller in an entirely different direction. The interviewer had opened up a sensitive area, and the teller had been prepared to answer honestly, but as there was no support forthcoming, the subject was dropped. While there might not be much you can say, you can convey empathy through your eyes and your body language, and with a thoughtful silence, empathy, and acceptance, you encourage the teller to recount both the joys and the sorrows of his or her life.

There are sensitive areas in everyone's life, and you might stumble on one by accident. One person might have a life-long feeling of inadequacy about a lack of formal education, and another might relive painful periods of self-doubt. When one really explores the past, one remembers the roads not taken as well as the decisions made. Every life has its share of pain, suffering, and the loss of loved ones. As the interviewer, all you can do is to listen with both your mind and your heart.

The teller's right not to answer

Listening with your mind and heart means being aware when the teller really doesn't want to answer a particular question. Everyone has areas of his or her life that are so personal that they are not to be shared, especially in a recorded interview. Although you may be curious and are asking questions with sensitivity, always be prepared to change the subject if you have touched on a person or memory that the teller doesn't want to discuss. This is discussed further in Chapter 8.

The interviewer's aim is not to challenge the teller's memory or point of view, but to provide the opportunity for a full exploration of the person's life.

But remember that recognizing the teller's right to privacy doesn't always mean that you should avoid asking certain questions! From my own experience in interviewing my father, I know that his silence about one area of his life didn't mean that he was unwilling to discuss it. It merely meant that he thought I wasn't interested.

Occasions for editing as you interview

Marriages and families can cause pain and bitterness as well as joy. Although it's important for people to express these feelings, a recorded interview may not be the best time. I'm reminded of a woman who still holds a great deal of anger towards the man she divorced some 20 years ago. When her daughter interviewed her for a recording, she began to express some of this anger, and was very critical of her ex-husband. The daughter, who had maintained contact with both parents, became extremely uncomfortable with this, and stopped the tape. She told her mother how she felt, and pointed out that the tape would be heard by the grandchildren in the future. The mother agreed that it was inappropriate. So they rewound the tape, and redid that part of the interview. Both people should keep in mind that the tape will be heard by others. While some opinions are fine when expressed privately, perhaps they don't belong on this kind of taped interview.

Keeping on track

No matter how well prepared you are, the interview will follow its own path in ways that you could not have expected. The teller might repeat him or herself, or follow a train of thought far from the path you were trying to set. Your job is to gently guide the conversation back to the questions you were asking. Digressions are often interesting, but you will want to keep the interview on track. For example, if you are interviewing an elderly person who loses his way, or rambles on, you might have to interject a comment such as, "Before we follow that idea, let's go back to your childhood," and gently take more control of the conversation.

Different ways of remembering

Sometimes the teller recounts a story which you remember too, and your reaction is, "That isn't how it happened at all!" Memory does play tricks on us, it's true. But it is equally true that the interpretation of an event depends on your perspective. If you remember an incident a certain way, it is not at all certain that your father will remember it the same way. Even siblings remember the same event very differently, and it is not a matter of conscious distortion but of point of view. So it serves no purpose to question a person's memory unless you are looking for very factual information.

Someone who recorded her family stories illustrates this point about her two aunts. "One of them lives in a retirement home. She loves it. She has friends around her, she has good food and lots of it. She's worked hard all her life and now can sit back and enjoy herself. And she feels sorry for the aunt who won't go into the retirement home because she has to do everything for herself. This aunt lives in an apartment and is an apartment manager. People of all ages come to her door every day. She has an interesting life in the middle of town. And she feels very sorry for the aunt who lives in a retirement home. I would talk to one aunt about her childhood, and she would tell me about certain incidents. Then I would go to the other aunt and ask her about the same incidents. Well, of course, I got two different stories, every single time. Even the details were different. The story line they had in common: It happened a certain time of year, a certain number of people were involved, there were certain important details. But the perspective and the emphasis changed with the teller. That's why it's so important for people to tell their own stories, because that perspective is unique. No one can repeat your story. No one can tell it like you can."

Memories are not like tape recorders on which everything we ever did can be played back.

No matter how well you know the teller, it is a good idea to make a written outline of questions beforehand to give the interview structure and to give both you and the teller confidence.

Taking breaks

Although you will find the interview stimulating and enjoyable, it will also be exhausting. To pay attention and listen deeply takes a lot of the interviewer's energy. And reaching back into the past for memories and answers to questions is tiring for the teller. So make sure that you stop when your energy begins to flag, or when you see the teller begin to get tired. You can take a short break, get up and stretch, have a cup of coffee, or plan to continue the following day. You will both come back to the project refreshed and ready to pick up where you left off.

Shaping the interview

There are an infinite number of questions to ask someone who is reflecting on his or her life: questions about genealogy, biographical details, questions about what life was like "in the olden days," about attitudes, values, philosophy, world events, and famous people that might have influenced them. Because every person is unique, each interview will be special; like a kaleidoscope, the many pieces that make up the teller's life will fall into a unique pattern. That pattern will depend on your interests, those of the teller, and the relationship between you. Each recorded interview will tell its own story. While following a roughly chronological path, you can make side excursions and digressions, but still maintain a sense of direction and purpose. As the listener, you can help shape the conversation so that it has a strong beginning and an effective ending that ties things together in some way.

Beginning with details of the teller's parents or grandparents is one way to revive personal memories which are not often talked about. Most people like to reminisce about their grandparents, and it starts the interview at a distance slightly removed from the teller. At the same time it encourages the teller to feel comfortable with you, and to trust that you know where you are going with your questions. This trust is essential to establish at the outset of the interview. Once you've established some of the facts—who the ancestors were, where they lived, and what they did for a living—you can ask some more personal questions. What kind of people were they, how did the teller relate to them, what were some of the particular stories that he or she remembers about them? Through this kind of discussion, you learn as much about the teller as about the ancestors.

Now you're ready to ask the teller some questions about his or her own childhood, school years, the social and political context in which the teller grew up, jobs, marriage, family life, and so on. Wherever possible, ask for stories and anecdotes to give color and texture to the memories.

Although you might use some of the sample questions in Chapter 14, you will want to ask questions that are specific to the person you are interviewing. For example, a man who could make or fix anything he turned his hand to told quite a funny story about an accident he had when he was a teenager driving his father's car. He fixed the car himself, but found that he had put the gears in backwards! Asked about when he started to tinker with things, he then related a lovely anecdote:

"In my upstairs attic I got an old phone and hooked it up to the phone system. My parents didn't know. It didn't have a dial, so I made a Morse key—that's all you need for dialing, I determined by experiment. So I could dial out with that. And I could listen in on the phone while they were talking, as well as call out. But the people from the phone company came out, asked if they could inspect the property, and my mother said "Yes." They went down, and found a wire. They asked where it was connected. My mother said, 'Well, I don't know, we never put any wire there.' 'Well, somebody did,' they said, and they followed it up to the attic. So my family found out that I had a phone. I've always been like that, I think."

We tend to forget those aspects of our lives that no longer fit with our current image of ourselves.

The interview's length

It's impossible to say at the outset just how long an interview "should" be. So much will depend on the state of the teller's health, his or her willingness to explore the past in detail, and the relationship between you both. Even one hour of tape will be precious beyond words for the future; on the other hand, you may find that one or two hours barely scratches the surface of what the teller has to say. Generally, the total interview, recorded over several sessions, will range anywhere from one to five hours. Any longer than that, and no one will ever be able to listen to the whole interview!

Certainly, if you find on the first day that the conversation is going to extend longer than two hours, suggest that you come back the following day at the same time. As well as giving you both the opportunity to recharge your (and the tape recorder's) batteries, it will also give you some time to reflect. Often, delving into the past raises all sorts of forgotten memories. Very likely you will find that the process of reminiscing has jogged the teller's memory, so that you will greet each other the next day with freshly remembered anecdotes and questions.

Set the time for the interview for when the teller's energy level is highest and try to ensure that you won't be interrupted.

Ending the interview

As the interview moves into the present, give some thought to how you will want to bring the tape to a close. Although in a sense the interview is intended as a legacy, the teller is not at the end of his or her life, and you don't want to suggest that all the important parts of the teller's life are in the past. You might ask some general "looking back" questions, but be sure to ask some "looking ahead" questions, as well. It's very important, no matter how intensely emotional the interview has been, to end on a positive note, and to leave the teller feeling good about the experience. And when it's over, you might decide to add the next installment a few years down the road.

CHAPTER 8

Family Secrets

The older I get the more secrets I have, never to be revealed and this, I know, is a common condition of people my age. And why all this emphasis on kissing and telling? Kisses are the least of it.

—DORIS LESSING

When we talk about telling family stories, the topic of secrets inevitably comes up, and questions arise as to how to deal with them. As the teller, how do we protect our privacy? Or, conversely, can we use this opportunity to unburden ourselves of something we have hidden but now want to talk about? As the interviewer, do we have the right to probe into areas we suspect are secret? How should we react when previously untold stories are revealed?

Just as every person has secrets, every family has secrets as well. There are countless reasons for keeping something secret. What one individual or family feels it has to keep secret might be talked about openly by another. Some of these secrets are quite benign and belong only to the person or people who are directly concerned. Others are lethal, capable of doing a great deal of damage within a family and sometimes beyond.

In discussing this emotionally charged area of human experience, my point of view is not that of a therapist. As we have seen in previous chapters, interviewing older family members about their lives can be very therapeutic, but the purpose of recording family stories is not to discover ways of exposing the secrets of the teller. Instead, I

89

A single snapshot literally contains a whole novel.
—Timothy Findley

want to look at ways that it may be cathartic for older people to talk about things that they may have felt reluctant to discuss before, and to establish some common-sense guidelines for dealing with such secrets that might be useful for life story interviewing.

Right to privacy

When my younger son was in his graduating year of high school, he and his friends were often out late on weekends. One Saturday morning, I was delicately probing: "So who were you with? Where did you go? What did you do?", trying to find out as much as possible without appearing too intrusive. When I realized I had probably asked one too many questions, I stopped and said, "Jonathan, I hope I'm not being too nosy." "Don't worry, Mom," he said blithely, "I only tell you what I want you to know."

That's true of us all. We constantly make judgments about what to reveal to the people in our lives and we are more open with some people than with others. Some people are talkative by nature, while others are more reticent about things they regard as private matters. Families, too, differ greatly in the openness of their communication. If a person has many secrets, he or she isn't likely to agree to an interview in the first place. But in any family story interview, there will certainly be areas of the teller's life that aren't known to the interviewer.

Although it seems the fashion these days, if one is to judge by T V talk shows and popular magazines, to talk openly about anything and everything, I really don't believe that it is incumbent on an individual to share everything about his or her life. Being honest with someone does not necessarily mean revealing details of personal experience that one doesn't want to talk about. People have a right to privacy, if they wish it.

The family story interview isn't an interrogation; it is more a gentle guiding of an entire life story into a few tape recorded hours. You might say to the teller, "I'm going to be asking questions to help you remember stories and experiences in your life. If you don't want to talk about something in particular, that's perfectly all right." That would have helped assuage the fears of the 92-year-old woman whose granddaughter wanted to interview her. Her two questions were, "Do I have to answer all the questions?" and "Do I have to tell the truth?"

Make sure the teller knows he or she isn't obliged to answer any and all questions. However, a caring interviewer will always try to create an atmosphere of trust in which the teller feels safe talking about personal issues, perhaps for the first time. And as we shall see, the interview may provide an opportunity for the teller to reveal things previously kept secret.

Harmless and harmful secrets

A secret can be said to be harmful when it becomes a burden to the teller, or starts to affect others in the family.

It's important to differentiate between simple issues of privacy, and harmful secrets. When a person chooses freely to keep something private, it is usually a harmless secret. In an interview, a mother might not speak of relationships she had before marrying her children's father, as a matter of privacy.

But other secrets kept within families are born out of pain, fear, or shame. Children might grow up in a family in which there has been the shame surrounding a bankruptcy, or the pain of the death of an infant. Thinking of these events provokes strong feelings, and so the family protects itself by keeping the story hidden from the outside world. If an interviewer is aware of such a "hidden" story, it is a good idea to ask ahead of time if the teller wants to talk about it in the interview. Sometimes, with the passing of years, the pain has lessened, and it is a relief to give voice to the secret.

A harmful secret is created when there is coercion to keep silent,

inflicted either by another person or by shame and prevailing morality. For example, when a child is sexually abused by an adult and told that "this must be our secret," it is clearly a toxic and destructive secret with consequences that can last a lifetime. When a young unmarried woman becomes pregnant and is sent out of the community by her censorious parents to have her baby, her resulting sense of shame will definitely affect her in the future. When the alcoholism of a father or the suicide of a mother is denied or covered up, the children live with a secret that will haunt them until it is brought out into the open and demystified.

This demystification can take place in a life story interview if the interviewer is sensitive, open, and non-judgmental. The job of the interviewer is to enable the teller to tell the story. It is not to put the teller on the spot, challenge, or criticize, but rather to listen with empathy and to stay with the story.

Who owns the secret?

In family history interviews, it is important to think about who has the right to tell a secret, and what happens in the interview if secrets are revealed.

Secrets can be held by one or more people. If it is what we have called a harmless secret, a matter of privacy, then it is up to the person concerned to decide how to react to questions about it. Georgia, a woman in her thirties, was preparing to do an interview with her father. She knew that her father had had a short marriage before he married her mother, but that he never talked about it. She was unsure whether to ask him about it, or whether she should find out more about it first. Georgia also planned to interview her father's elder brother, with whom she was on close terms, and wrote me to ask whether she should ask her uncle about her father's first marriage. Upon consideration, it seemed clear that it would be improper to ask the uncle to tell stories about his brother; it would be

far more open and above-board to let the father tell his story himself.

She decided not to ambush her father with questions, but to tell him ahead of time that she wanted to know more about those years of his life. In this case, the father said that he would prefer not to talk about it, that it had not been a happy time for him. The daughter had to accept that decision.

Sometimes, however, the teller will welcome the opportunity to talk about things that have been kept hidden for years. If that is the case, the interviewer will have to use all his or her listening skills to judge when to ask a question, how much detail to ask for, when silence is appropriate, and how to take the teller to a point of resolution with the story. There are really no hard and fast rules for this; it is an intuitive process. The important thing, as we have said, is not to be judgmental or to retreat from the story, but to be accepting and open.

Revealing harmful secrets

We now know much more than we used to about how some issues can have repercussions in the next generation. Innocent victims of destructive and secretive behavior, such as alcoholism or abuse, have the right to know how such things might have affected them.

One of the most glaring and tragic examples of the destructive nature of secrets is in the unconscionable physical, emotional and sexual abuse of Indian children in the church-run residential schools in Canada. Although the abuse occurred several generations ago, the effects on succeeding generations have been devastating in terms of social dysfunction. Dealing with it involves storytelling by the older generation, and bringing secrets out into the open is a first step towards taking away the shame and hurt that surround them.

How revelations such as these are handled depends very much on the individual teller and listener. It may be wise to consult a professional therapist to provide structure for such an interview to help deal with the strong emotions that will result from such revelations, for both the tellers and the listeners.

If the interviewer knows that the teller will be revealing painful or emotional secrets, the interviewer would be well advised to prepare for hearing them. Research into a situation can be very helpful. For example, in the case of the residential schools, each teller's story will be unique and personal, yet there is a common pattern to the stories, and the interviewer can prepare by reading some of the testimony of others. The telling of these difficult stories is made easier by knowing that others have similar experiences and have lived with the same secrets. Group support is a valuable part of healing.

Demystifying secrets as children grow up

An interview with a parent can be a splendid opportunity to ask some questions that haven't been asked before. Many children grow up thinking that there are areas of life they shouldn't ask about, and they leave home without asking questions that might be easily answered. As a parent, I find that there are certainly areas of my life that I haven't discussed with my children, not because I don't want to, but because it wasn't appropriate when they were little, and the opportunity to do so later has not yet presented itself. An interview might be the perfect occasion for telling those stories or talking about those issues.

A woman in her fifties wrote to me after interviewing her mother:

> During my childhood in the '50s and early '60s, the attitude to children was quite different from that of the '80s and '90s. Children were "protected" from hearing about difficult issues like illness, friction among adults, traumatic experiences. Things were sometimes hinted at but not fully explained and there was. At least in my perception, no invitation to ask questions. So things were left unsaid or only mentioned in passing.

... Secrets usually reveal a family's vulnerabilities.
—Monica McGoldrick

For example, I had no idea about my Jewish roots until I went to Israel at the age of nine to visit my grandfather. Nor had I any idea that my grandparents were divorced. I was left with a feeling that there were things I couldn't even find the questions for and the sense that I should have known anyway.

In the interview with her mother, the daughter was able to finally find the questions and answers she was looking for, and to understand not only what happened in her parents' lives, but why it happened, and how her mother felt about these events. The secrets were explained and demystified once the daughter was able to ask the right questions.

How and when are secrets told?

I have many examples of interviews with people who, as they get older, want to talk about a particular part of their lives which they have not yet discussed. Telling an old secret in an interview can be a cathartic experience, because the secret is no longer as dangerous or as damaging as it once was. When the context for the secret is known and it is explained in terms of the situation that the person faced at the time, the secret can often be quietly laid to rest.

As years pass, our ideas about what is "shameful" change. Whereas it was once unheard of for an unmarried woman to keep a baby, we now provide a lot of support for single mothers. It used to be a source of absolute dishonor to have to declare personal bankruptcy, but it is much less so now. These are no longer areas of dark secrecy.

One woman in her seventies talked to me about the taped interview she was about to do for her four children and her grandchildren. She told me about a relationship she had before marrying, which was very important to her. The relationship was never really resolved because the young man in question went to serve in World War II, and she never saw him again. When she married, it was to a

If you are well prepared for the interview, and look forward to it in a positive mood, it is likely to go well. However, it will never go exactly as you anticipate!

95

man whom she regarded as a good friend, but it was not like the romantic love she had lost. She worried that if she talked about her first love, the children would think that she didn't really love their father.

Her question to me was whether or not she should talk about that first relationship on tape. I suggested that she play it by ear, and if she felt comfortable, she should talk about it. During the taping, when she was talking about that time in her life, it seemed quite natural to talk about this special relationship. Afterwards, she told me that she needn't have worried. In fact, the children knew more than she supposed, and were happy to have the whole story before them. It gave them a greater sense of what she was like as a young woman, and made a touching story of wartime romance.

Here's another story. Ruby, a woman in her early thirties, goes to Barbados every couple of years to see her family. Every time, her grandmother tells the family stories, in the same way, using the same words. Ruby's grandmother tells about the birth of Ruby's mother, who was the eldest of eight children, and continues down the line. Recently, Ruby went to see her grandmother, taking her two-year-old daughter for the first time, and this time Ruby told her grandmother the story of her daughter's birth. The grandmother's voice changed, and she said, "Have I told you about Sally?" It turned out that Sally was her first-born, who died when she was three years old. There was also another child who died at birth. These two deaths were a family secret, known only to Ruby's mother, who was born shortly after Sally died. Ruby says that her grandmother was able to break the silence about these two children because of the presence of a beautiful young great-granddaughter who reminded her of Sally.

As we have seen, secrets can be revealed in life story interviews for many reasons: to set the record straight, to unburden oneself of a painful memory, or simply because times and social mores have changed over the years, and it is no longer a source of shame, guilt, or embarrassment to talk about what has been kept secret.

Role of the interviewer

As we have already discussed, the role of the interviewer when dealing with secrets is the same as it is in the rest of the interview: to be a non-judgmental listener, and to gently guide the conversation with sensitive questions.

It is possible that the teller will be able to recount secrets with equanimity, but revelations are likely to be accompanied by tears, anger, and pain, as the teller relives the experiences and the emotions that surrounded them. The interviewer should try to be comfortable with such emotion. Rather than saying, "Don't cry," or offering immediately to turn off the tape recorder (thus suggesting that showing emotion is something to be avoided), just sit quietly with the teller, keep eye contact, and indicate that you are not afraid to hear the emotion. It's likely a mistake to say, "I understand how you feel," because you probably don't. Your presence and questions have allowed the teller to reveal the secrets, and often the best approach is to convey non-verbally that you understand that telling the story is difficult.

It's important, however, for the teller to remember that the conversation is being taped, and so the interviewer should clarify that the teller wants the story on tape if it is a sensitive matter. The teller may feel comfortable, recounting a story to the person asking him questions, but less comfortable at the thought that others will hear the tape. If that is the case, the interviewer has several options. You can agree right away, and just not tape it. Or you can say, "Well, why don't we just leave the tape recorder on while you tell me about it, and I'll stop the tape at the end of the story. If you still feel that you don't want the story on tape, I'll erase it right away." Chances are that the story will be just fine, and the teller will be happy to have it "on the record." On no account, however, should a story be taped surreptitiously.

The more attentively you listen, the more the teller will want to tell you.

97

If, with the agreement of both teller and interviewer, the interview is used as a framework for talking about sensitive and secret areas, then the interviewer comes with a very clear agenda—to uncover the circumstances and details of the secret.

In one case a young woman of Hungarian origin found a photo of her grandparents on their wedding day. They were shown standing under a "chupah," the canopy over a Jewish wedding. And for the first time in her life, she realized that she was Jewish. Her parents, survivors of the concentration camps, were not religious, and had never told her about their Jewish heritage. Their motives for not telling her were really to protect her. They felt that they were starting a new life in North America after the war, and wanted to put the past behind them. And they were never entirely convinced that anti-Semitism wouldn't, at some time in the future, affect their children.

When the daughter found the photo, the parents explained why they had kept their Jewish heritage a secret. But this was clearly just the tip of the iceberg. The daughter had many more questions about the past, and asked her parents if she could record an interview with them, and they agreed.

The daughter prepared for the interview by reading all she could about Hungarian Jews during the World War II. She realized that it was not uncommon for European Jews who immigrated to North America to try to erase their past. But she still felt that the story was important, both for her and for her children.

In doing the interviews with her parents, the young woman tried to keep calm, although she was in emotional turmoil. Her entire sense of who she was, and who her family was, had to change. But as her parents felt free to tell the whole story, the story of their life in Hungary before the war, the horrors of the war, how they survived, the tales of people they loved, and finally why they chose to hide the fact that they were Jews from their own children, they felt liberated.

Every life is unique; no one has ever lived a life exactly like yours.

There were many emotional moments in the tape recording, and the interview marked a turning point in the relationship between the parents and their daughter. The parents gave the gift of roots and identity to their daughter, and the daughter was able to free her parents from the demons that haunted them by bringing them to the light of day.

Everybody has a public life, a private life, and a secret life. The public life is what the world knows of us; the private life is what our family and friends know of us. Sometimes our secret life is simply a kaleidoscope of pleasant, personal memories, which can nourish and sustain us and which are ours alone. But sometimes the secrets are harmful to us or others, and can poison our relationships with those we care about.

If there is a secret which the person who "owns" it wants to tell, a family story interview can provide the framework for telling it. The interviewer can prepare by knowing as much as possible beforehand about the circumstances. After that, it's simply a matter of asking questions that clarify and permitting the teller to talk in an atmosphere of trust and safety. Above all, the job of the interviewer is to listen with the heart, not merely the ear. If a life story interview is carried out with sensitivity, the highest ethical considerations, and respect, the telling of dark secrets can lead to healing. It can be a springboard to move out of the cycle of secrecy to an area of insight and understanding.

CHAPTER 9

Preserving the Tapes

*I've kept (the photographs), of course, because
something in me doesn't want to lose them, or perhaps
doesn't dare. Perhaps they're my totems, or contain a
portion of my spirit. Yeh, and perhaps they are exactly
what they seem to be—a jumbled mess of old
snapshots which I'll still be lugging along with me
when I'm an old lady.... I keep the snapshots not for
what they show but for what is hidden in them.*
—MARGARET LAURENCE

At this point in the process, you probably feel an enormous sense of
accomplishment. Planning and carrying out the interview has involved a great deal of energy and thought for everyone involved, and
now there is justifiable pride and satisfaction that the last question has
been asked and answered. However, the interviewer's work is not
over yet. When you get home with your bag of tapes, there are a few
things to do before you put the tapes away:

- Label each tape carefully, with the date, the name of the
  person being interviewed, the name of the interviewer
  (and videotaper, if there was one), the place, and
  particularly the order of the tapes.

- Punch out the tabs at the back of the cassettes to ensure that the cassettes can't accidentally be erased or recorded over.
- When you have the time, put the tapes into a playback machine, and make a rough outline of the topics covered on each tape, particular stories that were told, and the dates those stories occurred. If you set the tape counter at zero at the beginning of the tape, you can jot down the points on the tape where these stories occur. Since you cannot possibly cover everything, just concentrate on the highlights. Type or write out this outline, and glue it onto the cassette case. Here is an example of the outline of an interview with H.M., some of which appears later in this book.

TAPE NUMBER 1 SIDE 1

000	Born in England in 1906; family members
032	1911: Why family moved to North America
046	How father found property
102	Railroad trip from East Coast to West Coast
165	First winter in Bains Lake
198	Arrival at homestead site
218	Life on the homestead; the first cold winter
372	1912: Early school days a disaster
490	Happy memories of fishing and camping
529	1918: Story of solitary venture into Gold Creek country
610	Description of parents
682	Early love of carpentry

TAPE NUMBER 1 SIDE 2

000	Work in the sawmill at age 13; a dangerous place to work
109	Abortive career in surveying
204	Fishing trip to Gold Creek country at age 15
255	Another close call, with Mary on logging railway

It is worth making a little extra effort to ensure a good quality sound recording.

Making copies of the tapes

It is very important to make copies of the cassettes, whether they are audio or video. You will probably want to make several copies to give to other members of the family. Don't use a high-speed duplicating feature, but rather dub at regular speed in order to ensure the best quality.

Having more than one copy is also insurance against loss or damage to the original. Keep the original relatively undisturbed, and use a dub for playing, since repeated playing can weaken the tape. Also, if the playback machine is dusty or poorly maintained, the tape can be scratched or damaged. Store the original separately from the dubs. With these precautions, if something happens to one copy, you can always dub another from the original.

Reel-to-reel tape recorders are almost obsolete for home use, but most archivists of audio material transfer cassette tapes to quarter-inch reel-to-reel tape for permanent storage. They feel that by using the thicker tape (1.5 mil rather than 1 mil) they reduce the possibility of "print-through," which may occur when the tapes are stored for many years. To ensure the best possible chance of preserving the tape, check in the Yellow Pages for an audio recording service that will professionally dub your cassette onto quarter-inch reel-to-reel tape. A few archives have switched to DAT (digital audiotape), which seems to be the way of the future. But others are waiting until a universal or leading standard has emerged from the audio industry.

Making transcripts

Many people like having a transcript of the interview in addition to the tape. If you are looking for specific information on the tape, it is certainly faster to skim a printed copy of the transcript than to actually listen to or watch the entire interview. Transcripts are useful for people who don't have access to playback machines and for those

Sensory memories are very powerful; think of smells, sounds, tastes, and textures from your past.

Although some people seem to be natural raconteurs, everyone can tell their family stories.

who are away from home. And, of course, if you want to share the interview with someone who is hard of hearing, then a written transcript is best.

Transcriptions are very time consuming to type, but you may have someone in the family who is a skilled keyboardist and who is willing to take on the job. You might consider renting a transcribing machine which is essentially a playback machine with foot controls, that will allow you to stop, rewind, or slow the tape down as you work at the typewriter or computer. Or it might be worthwhile to take the tapes to a professional secretarial service. Make sure to use a copy rather than the original tape, as repeated stopping and starting, and constant high speed winding and rewinding, can damage the tape.

One caution: If the entire interview is transcribed word for word, it will contain the hesitations, unfinished sentences, colloquialisms, occasional grammatical mistakes, and particular syntax of the teller's speech. While these may be hardly noticeable when listening to a taped interview, they become a great deal more obvious when presented in print form. You may choose to edit it slightly for style, smoothing out the grammar, and omitting incomplete thoughts.

The interview transcript can be a highly valued document, particularly if it is accompanied by a few photos, perhaps ones that span the lifetime of the teller. A commercial copy center can do a beautiful job of duplicating the pages and photos, putting an appropriate cover on it, and binding it with your choice of bindings, making it something that everyone in the family will treasure, along with copies of the original interview.

Storing the tapes

Whether you have audio or video tapes, there are some things to keep in mind about maintaining them in the best possible condition for a long time:

- Avoid touching the tapes directly, as it is very important to keep them clean.
- Always keep them in their cases, as dust can damage both the cassettes and the playback machines. Store them vertically, with the empty reel up.
- Store them in a place with fairly average temperature and humidity. Avoid excessive heat (radiators, fireplaces), direct sunlight, and moisture. And if you listen to them on your car stereo, don't leave them on the dashboard in the sunshine!
- As the tapes are sensitive to magnetic fields, they should be stored away from your television set, stereo speakers, and all electric motors.
- If the tapes have been stored in a room with a different temperature than the area where the tape playback machine is kept, let the tapes sit for a few hours so that the temperature of the machine and the tapes is the same before you play them.
- If you plan to store the tapes for some time, it's wise to store them "tail out." Then, when you want to play them, rewind the tapes so as to flex them and get rid of any humidity that may have accumulated.
- Every year or so, take all the tapes out and rewind them, including the original which you have in safe-keeping. This will reduce the possibility of print-through from one layer to the next. And besides, you might enjoy listening to them or watching them again!

105

Family and Other Uses of the Taped Interview

Wisdom springs from life experience, well-digested.
—ERIK ERIKSON

If this book has encouraged you to finally set aside the time for capturing your family's stories on tape, you should feel proud and satisfied. At last, those fragments of stories you remember being told as a child are in a complete and coherent form. In addition, you may have learned a good deal about the teller in the process. Those tapes are very special, and certainly unlike any others in your tape collection. But you may be asking, "What can I do with the tapes once I've made them?" Some suggestions follow.

Family uses

- Don't underestimate how delighted other people will be to have copies of the tapes as birthday, Christmas, or Hanukkah gifts. If you value having your parents' life stories on tape, chances are that your siblings, cousins, aunts, and uncles will, as well.

- Excerpts from the tapes can be played on occasions that honor the teller—anniversaries, retirement parties, and birthdays. For example, on the occasion of your parents' wedding anniversary, the guests could hear your parents describing how they met and courted. Or when your mother retires from a career as a nurse, you might play a part of the tape where she talks about nursing school and her first jobs.

- Photo albums can be enlivened by quotations from the tapes. Colorful stories or descriptions of people and places can be transcribed next to the relevant pictures.

- The stories from the tapes can be retold or presented in the form of plays or songs at family gatherings. One friend of mine involved his own children and those if his sister in the presentation of a play which he wrote based on the lives of his parents and grandparents. The play was performed at his parents' 50th wedding anniversary celebration to great acclaim.

- Stories gathered from the tapes can also be retold in eulogies at memorial services. The minister or rabbi conducting a funeral service might find that listening to the tapes results in a deeper understanding and insight into what made that person unique. Those attending the service will appreciate remarks that are clearly specific to that person. At a time of grieving, it is important to reflect on the positive aspects of the person's life. The tapes may contain stories that are appropriate in this context, and some may even make people smile through their tears.

It is quite possible that the value of the tapes will become most poignantly clear after the teller has passed away. You might not want to listen to the person's voice or see a videotape for quite a while after the pain of loss, but at some point it will seem right to play the

Asking follow-up questions, and giving the teller time for reflection, are keys to a good interview.

tapes again. Death is not easy to accept, and is certainly not something anyone likes to think about, but it is a natural part of the life cycle. Just as we want to capture images of our children before they grow up, so do we want to have the stories of our parents and grandparents before they die. And in most cases, they will want to tell us those stories as part of their legacy to us.

Special family interviews

Memories will trigger other memories if you are relaxed and allow yourself time.

Although the emphasis in this book has been on taped interviews with older people in their own homes, there are many other ways in which the same approach can be productively applied. The current passion for roots, and the growing awareness that family stories are of inestimable value to one's sense of identity, suggest that people of all ages and in many different circumstances can use the ideas that have been described.

TEENS INTERVIEWING THEIR PARENTS

Adolescence is the time when the generation gap can seem its widest and deepest. By accepting the clear rules of the family story interview, the parent gives the teen permission to ask important questions, and the teen listens without challenging or criticizing the parent. This might be a change of style for all parties concerned.

The value of taping the interview is that it provides a verbal or visual "snapshot" of a pivotal moment in family life. All parents know how fast time passes, how quickly children grow up, and a tape would capture that moment forever.

The interview could certainly open up many areas of discussion, as well as giving both the teen and the parent greater understanding of one another. A sense of family is particularly relevant to teenagers, as they are struggling to develop a sense of identity both within and outside their family. And conversely, parents, in reliving their younger years, remember how complicated life can be for a teenager.

At a time of life when young people look for role models other than (or in addition to) their parents, family stories can provide ancestors who are inspiring. A great-great-grandmother who fought for the rights of women to vote, or helped slaves escape with the underground railway, or a grandfather who was a member of a jazz band that toured North America—all can be a kind of guide and a spiritual resource treasured by that person's young descendant.

One of the most interesting questions for the teen to ask is, "How did you decide on your career?" When young people are making important decisions about the direction their lives will take, this area of careers and job choices is of vital concern to them. And it's an area where the weight of family expectations, as expressed through the family stories, can be both a show of confidence and a burden. A 40-year-old teacher always thought he had let his father down because he wasn't a rich businessman. But now he understands where those expectations came from. His father sacrificed a lot to bring his young family from Spain some 30 years before, and he saw economic prosperity as a sign of successful integration into North America. The teacher now wishes he had talked it over with his father when, at seventeen, he was making the decision to pursue his education. He feels certain that it would have led to greater understanding between them.

PARENTS INTERVIEWING THEIR CHILDREN

Our children are amazing creatures with their own perspectives, philosophies, sense of humor, dreams, and aspirations. Though we keep photographs to chart their way through childhood and adolescence, we may not make the time to talk to them about what is important in their lives, what they remember from early childhood, how family events have affected them. Why not take a couple of hours at various points in their lives, to interview your children, find out what they are thinking, and make a permanent record of it all for the future! This is certainly one circumstance for which a video recording would be preferable. (Imagine being able to present your

Look around your house for things that can help jog your memory and appear on videotape, if that is the medium of the interview.

109

Interviewing my mother was a shared adventure. I wouldn't have missed it for the world!
—MS

daughter with a special gift on her 21st birthday—a videotape or audiotape with short interviews you did with her every few years as she was growing up.)

Seniors' interviews with non-family members

Not all older people will be interviewed by an adult child or a grandchild. There are some relationships in which the patterns of noncommunication are too firmly established to be easily overcome. Or sometimes the geographical distance between parent and family is too great to permit an interview. And in many cases, either by choice or circumstance, the older person has remained single or has no children.

SENIORS' PEER INTERVIEWS

Because we are social beings, most of us have friends who are as important to us as our family. We know that being part of a community plays an important role in our emotional health. And, more and more, we are discovering that friendships play a role in our physical health, as well. People who are involved in supportive social networks of one sort or another are literally less likely to get sick than those who are not.

As we grow older, our social networks often change. People whose friends were connected with their work find that in retirement they establish new links and connections. Modern cities can be alienating and isolating, and so we seek friendships among people with common interests, ideas, and goals. Community centers and seniors' groups provide a place for people to meet, and get to know one another. And this getting to know one another includes getting to know about each other's past life experiences.

Programs based on the premise that taped biographical interviews have great benefits for both the teller and the interviewer could easily be run in community centers. The group would discuss the project, its aims and objectives, and the techniques of tape recording an interview. A brainstorming session would be useful to suggest topics or questions in addition to those outlined in this book. Then the group would divide into pairs, and would conduct two interviews, alternating the roles of teller and interviewer. Such a project would probably take several weeks to finish.

There are some clear advantages to peer interviewing. Someone of your age has lived through the same periods as you, and has perhaps a more visceral understanding of living through the Depression, or losing a loved one in World War I or World War II. Values have changed over the years, and you may feel more comfortable discussing them with someone of your generation who shares them. And sometimes it is easier to talk about your family with someone who is outside that family. The interviewer might ask more direct and objective questions than your own son or daughter, and you might feel less self-conscious talking about your past.

Taping such an interview allows it to be passed on to your family or friends—a marvelous gift, more valuable than anything you could possibly buy for them. Do consider, also, that most communities have public archives which welcome donations of audio or visual material with historical value. If you have memories of the community more than 50 years ago, if you worked as a logger at a time there were no chainsaws, if you have recollections of meeting famous historical figures, if you can describe the everyday chores of homemaking years ago, if you were a skier before there were ski lifts to take you up the mountains—the archivist might very likely want to have a copy of your tape.

HOSPITALS AND SENIORS' CARE FACILITIES

I recently visited a 70-year-old woman in the hospital. Until suffering a stroke three months previously, she had been completely independent, active, involved in her community. Now she was paralyzed on one side, confined to a wheelchair, and working very hard to learn to walk again. She said to me wryly, "When the nurses look at me, this is what they see. But it isn't who I was, or really who I am!"

Family and Other Uses of the Taped Interview

Think carefully whether you would prefer to audiotape or videotape the interview, but be sure to become completely comfortable with the method you choose before the interview.

CHAPTER 10

It's essential for everyone who works in a care facility to see their patients in the context of their entire lives. When they deal with their patients, they have to see them as people who once were young and active, with dreams and aspirations much like their own. That man, who sits in his wheelchair looking half asleep, was a conductor on the passenger trains that criss-crossed the continent. That slightly cantankerous woman, who didn't want to participate in the bingo game, was the first woman mayor of her town. They are at another stage of their lives now, but it is not the sum total of who they are.

People come into care facilities from all walks of life, from a myriad of different life experiences, from a great many levels of independence. They have experienced losses of one kind or another: of a spouse, of friends, of an aspect of their physical health, of the job that was so much a part of their sense of identity. They have left a home with which they were familiar, and a community in which they were at home, to live in a strange and sometimes sterile environment with perfect strangers, sometimes for a short period, sometimes for the remainder of their lives.

Memory and reminiscences play an important part in helping people come to terms with this period of their lives. By exploring the past, they are reminded of how worthwhile their lives have been, and are helped to transcend the limitations that they now face. By putting fragmentary memories of events or periods into the context of their whole lives, they see their entire lives as an integrated whole. By thinking about what has been important to them, what their values and philosophies have been throughout their lives, they are able to articulate the ideas that have guided them. By remembering challenges and obstacles that have been overcome in the past, they gain strength to cope with the future.

Professionals in geriatric care recognize the importance of memories in the well-being of older people. Reminiscing therapy or life review helps a person come to terms with the past. Trained therapists help the teller to achieve self-acceptance and integration by under-

standing the unique pattern of his or her life. Memories groups have a less specifically therapeutic orientation, but are designed to foster social interaction among the patients. Perhaps once or twice a week, for an hour or so, people gather to share their memories of a particular time, stage of life, or event in the past.

When we share our past accomplishments with others, when we laugh together over life experiences we all have in common, we tend to sit a little straighter, smile a little more, reach out to others a little more generously. And there's such an evident link between our emotional and our physical well-being, that it's safe to assume that increased self-esteem leads to better physical health, as well. In addition, ideas about the meaning of life and our own accomplishments resonate in the stories we hear others tell. A social worker in an intermediate care home for seniors told me that she finds some of the patients to be remarkably like herself—except that they've lived 30 years longer!

However, there are several reasons for considering taped interviews of the reminiscences of the patients, even if there is a memories group in the hospital. The one-to-one relationship of teller and interviewer (a social worker, hospital volunteer, or family member who comes in for regular visits) provides many of the benefits of a therapeutic relationship without having therapy as its goal. The questions are specifically directed to the teller, rather than directed in a more general way to members of a reminiscing group. Making tapes of the interview will both reinforce the importance of telling his or her life stories for the elder, and will be greatly appreciated by other family members.

Interviews with the terminally ill

A few years ago, a 40-year-old friend was diagnosed as having terminal cancer. His wife asked me to record an interview with him, as a legacy for her and their four young children. Although he was ini-

I'll never forget the interview I did with my dad when we went back to Ireland together two years before he died. Unfortunately, his voice is inaudible on the tape, because we did it in a car, and I just had a small tape recorder with a built-in microphone on my lap.

—TM

tially reluctant, because it was such a clear acknowledgment that he was dying, he finally stopped putting it off. So one warm summer's day we sat down together and recorded his memories, starting with his childhood. It was an intense and bittersweet experience, during which we did not dwell on his illness but on his life. Now, after his death, the tape is there as a legacy to his children. They can listen to his voice, they can hear him laugh, and they can hear him express his love and his hopes for them.

As people approach the end of their lives, no matter what their age, there is a deep need and a natural tendency to look back, to relive the high points, to reflect on the combination of choice and chance that took them on their particular life's journey. Taping an interview permits the teller to metaphorically put a frame around his or her life, to make that life into a story. Although it's not easy to talk about the past with someone who is dying, doing a taped interview can be cathartic for both the interviewer and the teller, and a loving legacy for others.

Interviews with elders in ethnic groups

There are special reasons for particular ethnic groups to preserve their elders' memories. For the elders, it provides a welcome opportunity to pass on some of their ideals, values, and history to the next generation. For the younger people, it provides a sense of roots and identity. For both generations, it strengthens cultural pride and awakens a sense of shared history. If a group has had to emigrate from another country because of political or racial persecution, or if its members have suffered discrimination at home, it has a strong reason to remind the succeeding generations of its history.

Most ethnic groups have their own associations, and many of them have libraries which contain books by and about people of the same culture. A collection of taped reminiscences of the group's elders would be a valuable addition. Oral history projects have been undertaken in many communities, notably in black and native Indian communities, and these can provide a model for others.

A few years ago, in Massachusetts, The Cambridge Women's Oral History Project was undertaken. Young high school women were trained to interview older working women of varying ethnic backgrounds. The focus of the interviews was transitions in women's lives. The aim of the project, according to a board member of the Oral History Center, was "to promote multicultural and intergenerational awareness and respect to challenge stereotypes through the relating of individual life stories." When the tapes were completed, they were indexed, and formed part of a slide-tape presentation. A visual exhibit was made which combined photos as well as stories from the tapes.

What were the results of the project? It allowed the younger women to take part in the definition and dissemination of history, while learning to value the richness of older women's lives; it allowed the older women to recognize the historical as well as personal significance of their own life experiences.

Often intimate family stories carry more power than several history books. In an interview, a 65-year-old German-born Jew described how the growing menace of Nazism affected him as a schoolboy.

Teller: I wasn't a very good mixer. I kept mostly to myself or was with my friend Walter who was in the same class. I didn't like the teachers at all. I remember one throwing a bunch of keys at me because I couldn't sing in tune. Of course, at that time, boys arrived in school in their Hitler Youth uniforms, and they taught race theory in school. Mornings started with "Heil Hitler" and the singing of Nazi songs. We were not allowed to participate in sports activities, and things got very unpleasant.

Interviewer: How many Jewish students were there?

T: My friend Walter was the only one besides me.

How you phrase your questions will affect the course of the interview. Thoughtful questions will yield thoughtful answers.

I: You must have felt the focus of all that anti-semitism that was growing in Germany at the time.

T: Well, I don't know whether we were the focus, but we felt it because there were just the two of us. Because we were Jewish we were called "Dirty Jew." Immediately one withdrew, because there was no way of hitting back. That wasn't a nice period at all.

I: Was it possible to switch schools?

T: I did. In 1938 I went to the Philanthropie in Frankfurt. But it was a very interrupted schooling, because all the teachers from the school were sent to concentration camps, and the synagogue was set alight. So I had an interrupted schooling there, as well.

The process of interviewing elders can give a voice to people of different nationalities and backgrounds who are traditionally underrepresented in the mainstream media of North America. When people of diverse racial and cultural backgrounds tell their life stories to others who want to hear them, those stories are validated by the experience, and their self-esteem is enhanced as a result. This holds true no matter what the ethnic identity of the culture might be: black, native Indian, Chinese, Latin American, or whatever. And it is a meaningful and affirming experience for the listener as well. A library in a community center, school, or public archive, with taped reminiscences of people from different ethnic backgrounds becomes a rich resource for others in the future.

Adopted children and their natural parents

Children who were adopted grow up with many questions about their natural parents. What do they look like? Do I resemble them in any way? What kind of people are they? What do they do for a living? Do I have grandparents, siblings, aunts, or uncles that I don't know about? No matter how happy and loving a home the child grows up in, wanting to ask these kinds of questions is very natural.

Reunions between adopted children and their natural parents are occurring more and more often. Sometimes these reunions are just enough to satisfy the child's curiosity, and sometimes they result in a longer and deeper relationship. If a child is curious about the natural parent's life, and if the adult is willing to be honest about the past, a taped biographical interview can be a practical and comprehensive way of dealing with a lifetime of unanswered questions. And, as we have seen, it would probably result in a deeper mutual understanding.

School projects
ORAL HISTORIES

The use of oral history projects in schools is becoming recognized as an important educational tool at both the late elementary and high school level. By conducting interviews with older members of a community, or with participants in a particular event in the past, students learn a vast range of things: they learn firsthand what life was like in a previous generation, they hear illuminating stories from ordinary people whose stories aren't often shared publicly, and they are also able to see that the person they are interviewing was once a child like themselves. The teller, on the other hand, invariably finds that telling those stories to a younger person is a validating and satisfying experience.

Listen with your ear, your mind, and your heart.

Doing background research, making appointments for an interview, preparing a list of questions, conducting the interview (which involves verbal as well as listening skills), writing a thank-you note to the teller, preparing a transcript, making a report—all these achieve educational aims enjoyably and result in a tangible product.

Because oral history in schools has rich possibilities, we explore it in greater detail in Chapter 11.

STORYTELLING

There is a growing realization that storytelling can play an important role in education. Along with the pure joy and pleasure that children receive from telling and hearing stories, they develop important skills

117

All I knew was fragments, disconnected stories, bits and pieces of the puzzle of Mother's life growing up in the Deep South. When I did the interview, the stories fell together and formed a whole picture.

—LS

in speaking, listening, and understanding. The last decade's renaissance of the art of storytelling has led many people to look within their own families for stories to tell. And taped interviews with older family members by schoolchildren can be very effective in discovering some of the elders' best loved stories.

In a series of workshops given by a professional storyteller to a multicultural group of fourth to sixth grade students, the goal was to teach the children how to collect stories from parents and grandparents, and then to tell them in front of others. As with the oral history project, there was a good deal of preparation before the students actually undertook the interviews.

The children first told stories from their own lives, and in the process, learned what the elements of a good story are: a beginning, middle, and end, some concrete details so that the audience can form mental pictures and hear, taste, or smell what is being recounted, something about what the characters feel, some dialogue, and unique expressions and gestures in the telling.

One ten-year-old girl first told her story this way: "On my first birthday, my Mom made me a dolly cake. Whenever someone came to the door I'd run to answer it and pull them over to the refrigerator, open it, and show them the dolly cake." Then the class asked her questions: "What did the dolly cake look like? How did you feel about it? What did you say to people when they came to the door? What did you feel about eating it?" After incorporating these details, the girl expanded and developed her anecdote into a real story, which she loved telling and to which the children enjoyed listening.

The children's next step was to approach a parent or grandparent for an interview, and to prepare a list of areas that they thought might elicit good stories. Since one of the purposes of the activity was to foster inter-cultural understanding and pride in each child's own heritage, they asked such questions as: "Why did you leave your native country? What was it like to come to this country?" as well as questions about the teller's childhood. They taped the interviews, so that they would not have to take notes, but could concentrate on asking more questions to fill out the stories.

After the interviews, the children talked about what it had been like. "It was neat to hear all the stories." "I liked the way my grandma talked about her childhood." "I never knew that my dad had gotten into trouble when he was a kid." "We all laughed a lot together when we were talking." "I learned how my dad met my mom." "My grand-dad said he felt like a star!" And there were other responses as well: "It was hard at first, because my grandma said she didn't have any stories. But then she got going and it was hard to stop her." "It was weird. I hardly ever talk to my grandpa alone, just him and me." "I felt a bit shy asking them questions."

The success of the interview depended on several things. The children needed to feel comfortable in the role of interviewer, taking control of the situation rather than falling into the more familiar position of being told what to do. And the older person had to show him or herself ready to allow the child to ask personal questions, to take each question seriously, and to try to respond honestly.

From the interview, each child took one anecdote, and reshaped it into a story, following the principles that the class had developed. They put their stories in writing, and practiced telling them to each other, and then to other classes. Finally, they invited their parents and grandparents to an evening storytelling festival, where they retold their family stories. It was hard to tell who was prouder or enjoyed the evening more, the children or their parents!

Other possibilities

There is really no end to the ways in which recorded family stories can be used. They sometimes form the basis for theater productions, as well as biographical or autobiographical books, and for films about specific people and periods of history. They can accompany museum and gallery shows by reflecting the voices and thoughts of ordinary

people. Labor unions, as well as corporations, industries, and professional associations can also record the reminiscences of people who have been a part of their particular group or movement.

Although we have emphasized the value to families of interviewing older people, the historical value of these tapes must not be overlooked. We have spoken of them as recorded stories, but that is not to diminish the more general interest that they may have for researchers and historians in the future. If this is the case, and you feel that there is valuable historical information in the tapes, do consider depositing them in a library or archive that has an oral history collection. One proviso: Before giving the tapes to anyone else, it is essential to get the written agreement of the teller in the form of a legal tape release which specifies how the tapes will be used and who will have access to them. The tape release is discussed more fully in the next chapter, and a sample is in the Appendix.

Whenever people tell stories from the past, they provide a glue that bonds the listeners with the tellers. And by illuminating the past, they empower those who follow to set their own course with greater confidence.

CHAPTER 11

Oral History in the Classroom

In youth we learn; in age we understand.
—MARIE EBNER VON ESCHENBACH

Educators find that using oral history with students of any age can be richly rewarding. This chapter will focus on some suggestions for teaching students to interview, and the myriad ways that teachers at all levels can—and do—make use of oral history techniques.

Although oral history is usually seen as part of a social studies curriculum, it cuts across the lines that separate academic disciplines. It also transcends the limitations of the classroom by fostering interaction between the students and people in the community. And every school can find topics within the community to focus on. If the school is in a farming region, students might look at agricultural developments by talking to farmers who have been there for a long time. If the community is centered around a particular industry, students could talk to some long-term managers and workers. Or an entire class might decide to talk to people who lived through the Depression, to get personal stories from that time.

The pleasure and rewards of doing tape recorded interviews with older people are hardly reflected in the rather dry and academic term "oral history." One definition of oral history might be a method of investigation that uses people and their memories to explore events

*My seventh grade
students all know about
the personal lives of
film stars. But ask them
how their parents met,
and few of them know.*

—LB

in the past. Oral history documents the feelings, perceptions, and firsthand recollections of people, including those who have traditionally been left out of historical inquiry: not only the rich and the powerful, but also so-called ordinary people. It therefore complements traditional sources of historical research and gives us another, more human perspective on events in the past. At another level it is simply talking to people, usually those older than oneself, about their lives, and employing some standard practices to ensure that the information is well documented.

Even children in the early elementary grades can, with some practice, become competent oral history interviewers, with projects tailored to their abilities and interests. By the end of grade school, students can carry out quite sophisticated projects. In most areas, students in elementary school have large blocks of time with one teacher, so several disciplines can be integrated and easily (and usually enthusiastically!) developed and pursued. For example, a class might do an oral history project of a particular event in the past. As well as learning more about the event than they could hope to find in books, the students will enrich their English skills and they can use what they learn in the oral history to produce art, poems, a drama, a book, or anything else that an innovative teacher and imaginative students can think of.

In high school, where students tend to have a different teacher for each subject, interview-based projects can be carried out in almost any class. Later in this chapter we will have a look at some of those projects, developed for students of various ages in diverse disciplines.

For teachers looking for projects that build academic, social, and technical skills in which students work cooperatively and have fun, oral history projects are ideal. Unfortunately, very few jurisdictions include oral history in the school curriculum, so teachers have to use their ingenuity and creativity to develop projects, and learn from each other.

A pioneering project in oral history started in 1966 in Rabun Gap,

Georgia, where an enterprising teacher named Eliot Wigginton motivated a group of ninth and tenth graders to interview elders in their families and the community. Interviews were collected about myriad subjects, ranging from planting by the signs of the zodiac, to ghost tales, to how to build log cabins. The results were published in a little magazine, which the students called *Foxfire*. The students' motivation, energy, and enthusiasm, and the overwhelming response to the Foxfire project made it a public phenomenon. The little magazine grew to have subscribers all over the world and resulted in a series of books, as well as a collection of artifacts, tapes, and photographs. In more recent years, the project has expanded to include video, radio, and record production. Foxfire's underlying philosophy is that students will acquire academic skills—as well as the self-confidence leading to further learning—by taking part in real life experiences that call upon those skills.

Some school districts have made oral history a successful part of the school curriculum. One project was undertaken within a school in Massachusetts, when a seventh grade teacher decided to introduce oral history principles to her students. Some elderly people regularly came to her school for a hot lunch at noon, but there had been very little interaction between them and the children. In fact, there may have been an element of fear on both sides. The teacher decided to change the situation by having her students interview the "lunchers."

The actual interviews were the culmination of a long series of steps. First, one brave girl interviewed the teacher in front of the class, without any preparation, and the class "brainstormed." Which questions worked? Why? Which didn't? What should the girl have asked? Out of this brainstorming session, the class developed an idea of what makes a good interview.

Next, the class decided on a special focus for the interviews. They wanted to know what life was like for the elders when they were 13 years old, and they wanted to learn something about the community they had grown up in. They were then able to develop a series of

This project made me realize that history isn't just dry facts, but it's about real people!
—Grade 7 boy

questions which would be used as a framework for the interview. Next, the students did some practice interviews with adults with whom they felt secure. And, finally, they interviewed the elders. In most cases, a close relationship developed. At the end of one interview, the teller began to ask questions of the student interviewer about her own family life! At the end of another, a man asked whether he could recite a deeply valued poem that expressed his philosophy of life.

The taped interviews were then presented to the library in a joyful ceremony which included the elders, the students, drawings by the students, memorabilia of the elders, lots of food, warmth, and laughter all around. The students felt that they had participated in a real process of discovery, the elders felt honored, and the community was enriched by the addition of the tape collection.

Benefits to students

It is well known that students are much more engaged when they are actively involved than when they are sitting passively, trying to absorb information from a teacher or a book. The challenge for teachers is to harness and direct the considerable energy of students in creative directions and encourage their natural desire to learn. A teacher can teach the specific skills needed to prepare for the interview, but after that it's up to the students to carry it through and make their own exciting discoveries.

So what are those specific skills? On a most basic level, the students are engaged in:

- researching the topic
- learning how to plan and carry out interviews
- learning communication skills, particularly the art of listening
- operating a tape recorder

- writing and editing
- oral presentations
- organization of ideas and materials

But there are also benefits in areas that are less measurable. Family-based oral history projects increase knowledge of and appreciation for one's own family and culture. When stories are shared by people of different backgrounds, they challenge commonly held stereotypes and promote cross-cultural understanding. Self-esteem is enhanced as students are proud to share stories they discover about their own background.

Involvement in oral history projects demands that students take control of their own learning. Even at a young age, students can experience the thrill researchers feel when they uncover a fresh piece of information or a new perspective. They become real historians, creating primary historical documents, making discoveries, and sharing those discoveries with others. Learning becomes much more meaningful when it is grounded in the families and communities of the students themselves.

As a teacher, I found it just remarkable to see how kids got motivated and learned in spite of themselves!

—SS

Benefits to teachers

Oral history is an educational tool that has proven to be successful in motivating students and teaching course content as well as academic, social, and technical skills. It both supports and augments the school curriculum and is extremely versatile; an oral history can be designed in almost any area, and the span of the project can range from a couple of weeks to a full academic year.

Some interesting research about how students learn history, suggests that it is not just an accumulation of facts. Rather, students have to learn to make judgments about the relative significance of events, and put them into some sort of moral framework. Oral history projects help them understand the human dimension—the circum-

stances that people found themselves in and the choices they made. They are much more apt to be interested in the topic if they can make an emotional connection with it.

A high school teacher in a large, urban, multicultural school, proposed an oral history project to her students, giving them the choice of two topics: war and immigration. The class, a group of rather recalcitrant 15-year-olds who gave the impression that they would prefer be doing anything other than sitting in school, objected least to the topic of war. By the time the project was finished, three months later, they were fully involved, proud of their work, and asked their teacher whether they could do another oral history project, this time focused on immigration.

Benefits to the community

Oral history builds important bridges between the classroom and the home, and between the school and the community. Since oral histories are usually done outside the classroom, parents are more likely to take an active interest in the project and its final outcome. In the case of family story projects, in which the students interview family members, the sharing of stories can lead to deeper understanding between people of different backgrounds.

The people asked to tell their stories generally feel honored for their particular knowledge or experience, and if they are living in a household without younger people, are likely to enjoy contact with the students. Sometimes the oral history project will illuminate the lives of community members in such a way that the whole community feels pride and validation.

An enterprising teacher can take the oral history project beyond the collection of audiotapes by having the students create something based on the content of the stories. Older students might produce a community play, a slide/tape presentation, or some other offshoot from the history. At this point the teacher might enlist the help of

someone in the community with particular expertise. For instance, a journalist might provide guidance on how to produce a small newspaper, or an artist might lend a hand with the creation of a mural or a quilt. Younger children might simply have a storytelling evening, where they invite their parents and the community members they have interviewed, and tell the stories they have heard. It is always a pleasure to see bridges being built and reinforced between school and community.

Steps in an oral history project
A. DEFINE THE GOALS AND FOCUS

The plan for an oral history project must take into account the age of the students. With younger ones, the teacher must take more of a leading role in defining aims and objectives. For older students, however, part of the excitement comes from the students themselves having a say in the topic and particularly the final outcome.

If your school is in a rural area, and there are older people in the community who have lived there and gone to the same school as the children, they can be a great resource. Younger children might simply want to interview the elders about their memories of the school. But high school students might choose to do something quite a bit more complex. They might, for instance, interview those same elders in more depth about their trades, their beliefs, their memories of the changes that they have seen over the years. The successful *Foxfire* project, described earlier, was very much a rural phenomenon, and took advantage of the skills and knowledge of the people in the area.

One of the first things to be decided is the focus of the interviews, the question of whether the interviews are to be biographical (covering the life history of the teller), or whether they are to center on a particular event in history, or whether they are to investigate specific topics (such as belief systems or occupations).

At this point, you'll have to think about whether you want the students to work in groups or individually. If the students are interview-

Along with the pure joy and pleasure that children take in telling and hearing stories, they develop important skills in speaking, listening, and understanding.

ing older people they don't know, they might be more comfortable going into the person's home with a partner. As the teacher, you will need to be conscious of safety, particularly in an urban environment. You may choose to invite the interviewees to come to the school to be interviewed, rather than have students go into their homes.

It might also happen that families are from ethnic or cultural backgrounds in which questions are not welcomed. For example, a family that has been forced to flee an oppressive regime might still feel uncomfortable or threatened by questions about their background. For these reasons, and as a matter of simple courtesy, the teacher should write a letter to parents clearly outlining the goals of the project and telling them precisely what the students' assignment is. A sample letter is shown in the Appendix.

I found out a lot from my grandmother about World War II that I hadn't learned in school.
—Grade 8 girl

B. BACKGROUND RESEARCH

The amount of background research the students can be expected to do will vary considerably, but no matter how simple the project is, some background research is always a good idea. An elementary school class investigating the history of transportation, for instance, might go to the library and look through old magazines to get a sense of the cars that their grandparents were driving in the 1950s. Older students interested in the same topic will use more sophisticated research methods, including computer searches, books, information from transportation museums, or possibly films and videos. These days, many high school students using the Internet are able to get more information than their teachers who grew up in the pre-computer age! You will find that this is an important part of the project, with students learning how to read, take notes, synthesize, and use background information to ask informed questions.

C. CHOOSING AND APPROACHING THE TELLERS

The names of people who could be good sources of information will come to you through word of mouth, and research. It can be quite a detective feat to track down people whose names appeared in newspaper stories of several decades ago. Seniors' centers and other relevant organizations, such as trade unions, are obvious places to go for sources. You might want to put a notice in a community newspaper, explaining the project and asking people with specific knowledge or backgrounds to volunteer to be interviewed. The older the students, the more they are able to take charge of finding the people they want to interview. It's wonderful how enterprising kids can be when they are excited about a project!

When you have a list of potential interviewees, it is a good idea to write, or have the students write, a letter (on school letterhead) that outlines the project and sets a date for the student to contact the person. It is rare that anyone declines a polite and sincere request to speak about themselves and their experiences.

D. THE PRE-INTERVIEW

It is important for the students to meet or at least speak with their subjects before the recorded interview. This breaks the ice, and allows both student and interviewee a chance to get to know one another. The success of the interview will depend somewhat on the rapport that develops between the student and interviewee, and the pre-interview is a chance to establish that rapport. The student should have some specific questions in mind to ask the teller. For example, if the interview is with a veteran of the Second World War, it is helpful to find out in the pre-interview where the veteran served, whether he was in a prisoner of war camp, and what his dates of service were. This information will enable the student to focus the research and questions that will be asked in the recorded interview.

The danger is of course that the interviewee will start to recount some terrific stories, and telling them before the actual interview might destroy their spontaneity later. Difficult though it might be, the student will have to be firm about not wanting to hear the details before the tape recorder is running.

Stories from the past are a glue that bonds the listeners with the tellers.

129

One way of organizing the pre-interviews is to have a casual get-together beforehand. A group of young Chinese Canadians who were going to interview Chinese Canadian war veterans, arranged to have a picnic together a few weeks before the interviews began. The resulting warm relationships led to more revealing interviews than would have otherwise been possible.

More formal oral history projects may use questionnaires with biographical data the interviewer can fill out when she meets the teller for the first time (see sample in Appendix). The questionnaire is useful if the data has to be the same for all interviews, and it's then easier for the interviewer to say, "I'd love to hear that story when we get together in a few days, but right now I have to fill out this questionnaire!"

E. TEACHING INTERVIEWING SKILLS

Most media-savvy students will immediately see the difference between a conversation and an interview. Rather than participating in the give and take of a conversation, the interviewer should try to be like a reporter; to focus the interview, and to have at least an outline of the topics to be covered. The student needs to be non-judgmental, ask good questions, and listen carefully to the answers.

Because listening is such an important part of the interviewing process, brainstorm with the students what it means to be a good listener. From their own experiences with friends, they will understand that listening involves:

- body language (eye contact, leaning forward, not fidgeting)
- not interrupting, but encouraging with smiles and nods
- asking follow-up questions
- keeping the interview on track
- giving the interviewee time to answer (permitting silence)
- listening for gaps in chronology, and making sure the story is told in its entirety

How one phrases questions is very important. We have already discussed general guidelines in Chapter 7, but here are some suggestions to help the students:

- Try to avoid "closed" questions, those that can be answered with a simple yes or no. Start questions with phrases such as "Describe …," "Tell me about …," "What was it like when … "
- Use prompts such as "And then what happened?" or "Can you tell me any more about that incident?" to encourage the teller to elaborate.
- Incorporate your research into questions. For example, in the case of the Chinese Canadian war veteran, you will have found out beforehand which branch of the armed services the veteran served in. It is more effective to ask, "Why did you choose to join the air force?" than a more general question.
- Keep questions simple, not double-barreled. For example, rather than asking "Where were you born, and can you describe your family?" ask one question at a time and make sure the teller has time to answer.
- Aim to get stories as well as facts by asking for elaboration about images and emotions. For example, when interviewing someone who has been fishing commercially for many years, the person might mention the danger of fishing in rough seas. The student could follow that up with "Can you remember a particular trip when you felt afraid? How high were the waves?"

The interview went smoothly. My great-grandfather didn't talk as much as I had hoped. I had to ask lots of questions. He's almost 100 and I'm amazed that he remembered as much as he did.

—Grade 12 boy

Try to have the students practice interviewing before they do the formal oral history. It can work well to divide them into groups of three, with an interviewer, an interviewee, and an observer of both questioning and listening skills. Give the students a general topic and let them formulate their own specific questions and carry out short interviews. They will learn that they already possess many of the qualities required of a good interviewer, for instance, curiosity, sensitivity, good listening skills, and the ability to be spontaneous and think on their feet.

F. MAKING AN OUTLINE

Once the students' interviewing skills are prepared, it is valuable to begin to think about the interview in more detail. Together with the students, generate an outline of questions and subject areas to be covered for the student to take along to the interview. For example, if the project is focused on the teen years of grandparents of the students, the topics might include everything from family relationships to music to hairstyles and dating. The students will have no trouble coming up with pertinent (and impertinent) questions. The outline should be seen as a guide, rather than a questionnaire. Each interview will take its own unique direction, depending on the individual experiences of the interviewee, the skill of the interviewer, and the relationship established between them. The outline will give the student a basic structure from which to work, and the confidence from planning the direction of the interview. It should also inspire confidence in the teller, as evidence that the student has given a great deal of thought to what he or she wants to ask.

Let the students know that it's a good idea to plan the beginning and ending of the interview with some care. At the very beginning, the student should identify the teller, the interviewer, and the date and place, before the opening questions to get the conversation rolling. Similarly, there should be a few closing questions that allow for some philosophical wrap-up of the topic. For instance, in the case of the oral history project about teen years, some closing questions might be, "What or who was the biggest influence on your teen years?" "Were your values and beliefs then different from now?" "In what way do you think your teen years prepared you for adulthood?" At the end it is

courteous to ask, "Is there anything you would like to add?" and then to thank the person for taking the time to do the interview.

G. TEACHING STUDENTS TO USE THE TAPE RECORDERS

One of the challenges facing a teacher who wants to introduce an oral history project is how to find enough tape recorders for the class to use. Students might bring tape recorders from home, but the quality will be extremely variable. One option is for students to share tape recorders, arranging the interviews for times that a tape recorder is free. Schools or school boards can sometimes make good quality cassette recorders available to teachers who request them. If the final product is to involve the tape recording itself, rather than just a transcript, it might be worth purchasing several tape recorders for use in the school.

Some guidelines for audiotaping are given in Chapter 5, but it cannot be stressed enough that practice is essential! Students should practice turning the tape recorder on and off, positioning the microphone, using earphones, and interviewing one another. They will enjoy mastering the new medium as they get used to hearing their voices on tape and handling the equipment. Here are some suggestions for class activities involving the tape recorders:

- Have young students sit in a circle, and pass the tape recorder and microphone around. Each student takes a turn telling a story about their name; how they got it, what it means, whether or not they like it.
- Have older children do mock media interviews with one another. One is the reporter, interviewing the fastest runner in the world, a famous rock musician, a TV star, or a scientist who has just made a world-shaking discovery.

H. WHAT TO DO WHEN THE INTERVIEW IS OVER

If the interviews will be used for any kind of public presentation or event, it's a good idea to have the interviewee sign a release form.

My mother started to cry when she told me about my dad in a prisoner of war camp in Vietnam. I didn't know what to say, but she liked talking about it to me. It made me feel important because I had never asked about it before. It had to do with real feelings, not just facts.

—Grade 12 girl

This simply gives permission for the interview to be used in a particular project. For ethical and legal reasons it is important for the interviewee to know exactly how the interview will be used. (See sample release form in the Appendix.)

Remind the students about standard care of the tapes when the interview is finished:

- Punch out the tabs at the back of the cassette so the tape cannot be erased.
- Label the tapes carefully with names and date. Number the tapes for easy identification.
- Make at least a summary of the tape's contents, as suggested in Chapter 9.

Have the students write a note of thanks to the tellers after the interviews. Oral history isn't a dry academic discipline; it's about human communication, and small gestures of appreciation and courtesy are as important for students to learn as the skills of interviewing and taping.

I. THE NEXT STEP

The interviews might be only the first stage in a more complex project. Here are some ideas for collaborative projects which have been done in classrooms around the world that incorporate oral history interviews:

- Publications that contain either a transcript or a synopsis of each interview
- A mock-up of a newspaper from a distant time or place, using information gained in the interviews
- A documentary audio program, edited from the tape recordings
- A drama written and performed by the students, built on the stories of people who were interviewed

- A quilt, composed of squares made by the students, each representing an image from their interviews
- A song, in which each verse contains some story or image gleaned from the tapes
- A mural made of images from the interviews
- Graphs or maps containing data revealed by the interviews
- A storytelling festival in which the students retell stories they have heard

J. SOME SUGGESTIONS FOR ORAL HISTORY TOPICS

Teachers excited about the possibilities of oral history projects have always found ways of incorporating them into the curriculum. The curriculum itself may suggest the topic; for example, if a high school class is studying the Depression, interviewing people who lived through the Depression would be an obvious complement to the text books. Teachers might also consider less obvious topics for oral history research. Here is a sampling of ideas for topics:

Family history
(interviews with parents or grandparents, including particular events, or turning points, or a general biography)

- Focus on "when you were my age"
- Focus on immigration. Put up a map that indicates where all the students' grandparents were born. Have the students each recount a story about a move their family made.
- Focus on war. Have the students interview a person in their family whose life was touched by a war.

Regional history
(interviews with pioneers, and others who have lived in the area for a long time)

- Focus on industries and occupations that have grown or declined
- Focus on the lives of the pioneers
- Focus on the history of particular landmarks or buildings

Cultural history
(interviews with people of various cultural backgrounds)

- Focus on holidays and celebrations, by interviewing a variety of people from different religions and ethnicities
- Focus on the art and culture of particular groups
- Focus on childhood games

Social history
(interviews about trends or movements that occurred before the students were born)

- Focus on women's history in a specific region
- Focus on the stories of trade unionists
- Focus on the significance of the 1960s

As mentioned before, even though oral history has been used principally in social studies and English classes, it is extremely versatile, and a teacher of almost any discipline can adapt it to his or her needs. Home economics teachers can design interesting projects about the changes that have occurred in homes and families over the years. Physical education teachers can have their students look at the way attitudes towards health and fitness have changed. Foreign language teachers can have their students conduct interviews with native speakers of the language they are learning on a topic relevant to those people. Teachers of ESL have found that they can encourage their students to write and talk in English when the stories come from their own personal experiences. Similarly, adult literacy classes often use personal and family stories as a basis for class projects. The possibilities are endless, and the rewards are great.

Dad was glad to do the interview. He'll do anything to get my marks up. At first I thought, "Boring, boring, boring." But when he started to talk I learned so much!
—Grade 9 boy

Genealogy and Family Stories

*When I found all my cousins, I found myself in many
reflections ... I found that my father was more than a
father; he was also a brother, an uncle, a son, a
grandchild and a cousin himself ... My cousins have
let me into their lives and their hearts, and they have
given their stories with generosity. This is what an
extended family does for you, either sideways or back
in time; it makes you less solitary and less unique.*
—PAULETTE JILES

The growth of interest in genealogy

People have always been intrigued by their ancestors; think of the
many references to family links between people of different generations in the Bible. And for many families, the family Bible is where
births, deaths, and marriages have been recorded. But in the last 20
years or so, there has been an explosion of interest in tracing the family tree. Some people attribute this to the publication of Arthur Ha-
ley's bestseller *Roots* in 1976, and the televised drama that followed.
Whatever the reason, many people have caught the genealogy bug,
and today genealogy is ranked as North America's fastest growing
hobby. There are innumerable books, magazines, and even profes-

sional genealogists who can help with the search for ancestors or living relatives. People engage in genealogical research on their own and then meet or correspond with other genealogists to share information, to exchange research methods, to boast about how far back they can trace their ancestry, and to trade tips on everything from computer programs to book bindings.

What's the reason for this passion? The answer probably is related to some of those factors that were discussed at the beginning of this book. Social mobility, immigration, and the rising number of single parent families means children often grow up far from older generations of their families. Researching a family tree, sometimes going back hundreds of years, gives one a sense of rootedness, of connection with past generations. You can come to see yourself as a link in a chain that stretches into the past, but also forward into the future, which in turn may provide a feeling of strength, purpose, and identity.

For Dolly, a widow in her seventies, doing genealogical research has allowed her to trace both her and her husband's families back to the 1600s. It has also opened up a whole new network of living relatives with whom she is now in close touch. Her father died when she was five, and she decided to go back to the town in Pennsylvania where he was born. "And with a name like Anderson, in that area, if you just blink you'll miss an Anderson walking by. I was there just meandering around, checking cemeteries, church records and so on, and I met some third and fourth cousins that way. Some of them invited me to their homes, just because I'm an Anderson too. People even told me I looked like them. You meet a lot of nice people that way."

Another genealogist, 50-year-old Gordon, had his interest sparked by seeing the names on the family tree in the family Bible, and wanting to flesh out the stories, to find out who these people were, and something about them. So he started with oral history, asking older members of the family what they remembered, and soon found himself in libraries and archives, trying to fit the family into social history and to see the family in a larger context. As well as having a huge data base of

over 4,000 names, Gordon says that genealogy has become "a passport to figuring out the lives of real people in different times and places."

For example, there is the military medal issued in 1851, which had been passed down for generations but for which no one in the family had a complete explanation. It gives the dates of the conflict as 1809–1814, the clasp indicates "Martinique," and writing on the rim tells that it was issued to Samuel Bailey of the 7th Artillery. Gordon started the search. "I went to a book of medals, and it told me that it was issued posthumously to men who had served on a British ship that was taking Martinique in 1809 from Napoleon. So then I went to British military records, and found that Samuel Bailey was discharged in the 1820s, as well as some correspondence from him regarding his pension. There was a reference to him as being from the Rideau military settlement in Canada. A search of history books told me that this was land given to people discharged from the British army following the War of 1812 between the Americans and the British, fought in Canada. Then I went to the land records and traced the ownership of the land, and was able to establish where he settled in Canada. When I was in London, I went to the public records office, and it told me in which parish and county in Ireland he was born. From the discharge records I even found that he had been a shoemaker, he was five foot nine with blue eyes, sandy hair and a 'fresh' complexion. Almost as good as a photograph."

The research itself, which can take many years, is richly rewarding. For those who become interested, or more likely obsessed, by their genealogical research, it's a kind of detective game, a personal challenge, and sometimes an all-consuming passion to identify as many relatives and ancestors as possible, and fill the family tree with names and dates. Genealogists enjoy searching through journals, cemeteries, municipal records, lists of ship's passengers, and newspapers to get clues and confirmation as to where their family came from. Each new bit of information is another piece of the puzzle. The puzzle is never entirely complete; there's always more to do.

I think it's important for you to see this so that you realize that who you are isn't necessarily all your fault. You can blame it on your gene pool.

—Michael Keaton
(My Life)

How do stories fit into genealogical research?

The story of each family's history is unique, and people derive a sense of connection and identity from learning about their history. Traditionally, genealogy has been concerned with the facts, verifiable and documented, about a particular family. But along with those facts come family stories, that make one realize that each name on the family tree is that of a real human being, with virtues and vices, and hopes and disappointments; someone, in short, who lived a real life. In the words of one genealogist, "You get names and dates, that's just the skeleton. To put flesh on the body, you need to get the stories about your family."

So the complete family history is comprised of both genealogical facts and family stories. For some genealogists, there has to be some kind of evidence that the story is actually true. The widow who found her Anderson relatives told me that one of the pleasures of that was to verify family stories. If a family story about a common great-grandparent came down through two different lines, then you could assume it was true!

If a person is embarking on a history of the family, a first step is to interview living family members to get as many facts and stories as possible.

A young man of 23 was trying to learn the story of his great-grandfather's emigration from England to Canada. He knew that his great-grandfather had grown up in a fairly well-to-do family. He also knew that this great-grandfather and his younger brother had homesteaded in Alberta in the early 1900s. What he didn't know was why they would leave a comfortable middle-class life for the hardships and uncertainty of life on the Canadian prairies. So he interviewed his own grandfather, now in his early eighties.

  T: Well, he was the second youngest of a family of five. His father owned a mill and a farm, and in typical English fashion, the eldest son inherited the mill, the next son the farm, the daughter married, and the two younger children had to shift for themselves. And so my father, after finishing grammar school, worked for a while in a bank, and that seemed rather a dead end job, so he looked for something different. By this time, my uncle had come out to western Canada, so he felt he might as well join him and see what the New World was like.

I. What did he plan to do?

T: Oh, farming, as all Englishmen did at that time. I should add that home in England was an old manor house, built in the time of Queen Elizabeth I, with lawns and tennis court and lily ponds, and a couple of maids, and a gardener, and so forth. And I stress this by contrast with the life he was soon to find in western Canada.

I. How did he get started?

T: He and his brother worked for an established farmer east of Edmonton. And in 1912, both my Uncle Herbert and my father got their homestead, which was a quarter section of land, and they trekked out from Hardisty 50 miles with all their worldly belongings, namely a couple of plodding oxen, a crate of chickens, a great big cheese and so forth, taking two days to reach their destination. And the first night when they stopped, they wondered, what about these chickens, they've been cooped up all day. Shall we let them have some exercise? Well, when they turned them loose, of course the chickens all ran off. My father and Uncle Herbert just couldn't round them up, and finally had to give up. But when the chickens had had their run then amazingly enough they all came back to the only home they knew, namely the crates. Then they continued on the next day and reached the sod shack, with the oxen and the chickens living in one end and them in the other.

I. Where exactly was this?

T. This was midway between Edmonton and Saskatoon, 12 miles south of the main CNR railway, in an area of good soil surrounded by sandhills. In England I'm sure they had never even

You can prepare by sketching a genogram, and thinking about the stories you know about various family members.

boiled water, let alone made their own bed. So here they were, two bachelors stuck out in the bald prairie, having to do all the work. But they survived, even though it must have been on pretty simple fare.

Through an interview with his grandfather, this young man learns not only the facts of his great-grandfather's emigration, including dates and places, but a great deal more about the social and historical context. An ancestor who died before he was born becomes a real person in his mind. And he also, not incidentally, has a well-recorded tape of his own grandfather's voice telling the stories with great gusto!

That's not the only way that ancestors become "real people." Dolly told me that her husband once came home to find her in tears with her genealogy charts open in front of her. She had just been looking at the information she had of a woman in her family who lived in 1875. Within one month, four of her five children had died in an influenza epidemic. The tragedy of this woman's loss moved her descendant to tears, over a century later.

As we have seen, family stories can emerge from genealogical research as well as from oral history. No matter how they are discovered, the result is that ancestors, previously just names on the family tree, suddenly become much more than that. We learn something about the circumstances in which they lived, the kind of people they were, the forces that shaped them, the choices they made. And, as one genealogist said, "It gives me the sense that I'm part of something, and I'm coming from somewhere."

Using a taped interview to convey genealogical information

Genealogists, as we have seen, can become quite preoccupied with their research. However, other members of the family may not share their passion to the same degree, and frustration may arise on both sides. The genealogist wants to convey the excitement of what he has discovered, and the rest of the family cannot understand the importance of a collection of facts about people long dead.

Samantha, a woman in her thirties, told me "My father goes into so much detail with his genealogy that we have all lost interest. It's beyond us, we just don't understand. And so he knows all about our family and just can't communicate it to us. In a way, we take him for granted, and don't give him credit. We don't try to share his excitement about what he's doing … I've often thought of asking him to give us a presentation—an evening where we would devote ourselves to listening to his genealogy."

When her father had a mild heart attack, Samantha decided not to put it off any longer. Instead of having her father give a presentation, she set up a video recorder, and conducted an interview with him, asking him to share what he had learned about the family in conversational mode. It was a great success, and gratifying to both Samantha and her father.

Digressions are often interesting, but you want to keep the interview on track.

Genograms: family trees that tell stories

The standard format for a graphic representation of genealogical research is the pedigree, or family tree. Taking yourself as the focal point, you chart siblings, descendants, and ancestors. The usual information is date of birth, death, marriage, and name of spouse. Obviously, with each generation one goes back, the family tree becomes more complex. At the same time, the type of information on a family tree is quite limited.

The genogram provides a new way to chart family relationships and themes and it has a lot of potential for people interested in family stories. Genograms were developed as a tool for family therapy. They are a graphic representation of relationships as well as individual characteristics and behaviors, and usually cover at least three generations. Using symbols and notations, one can chart patterns that repeat themselves through several generations, and visually show the emotional

relationships, occupations, illnesses, causes of death, as well as the stories of people's lives. Obviously, this means that a genogram is a good deal more subjective than a family tree, as it reflects both the teller and the interviewer's perceptions and perspectives. But for our purposes, it is infinitely more flexible and adaptable than the standard family tree, allowing the insertion of virtually any information in schematic form. The resulting chart can give fresh insights and perspectives and lead to questions an interviewer might not have otherwise considered.

The genogram was developed from the work on "family systems" pioneered by Dr. Murray Bowen in the mid-1970s. In *Genograms and Family Assessment* (1985), authors Monica McGoldrick and Randy Gerson describe the symbols and construction of genograms.

Although you can develop your own symbols, some of the most common universal symbols are:

- □ male
- ○ female
- ▣ ◎ focal person
- ⊠ ⊗ deceased
- Ⓐ Ⓐ adopted child
- △○ twins

Relationships are indicated by connecting lines:
Couples:

- □—○ married
- □--○ unmarried
- □—#—○ divorced

Connections between any two people:

- □══○ close relationship
- □∿∿○ conflicted relationship

Dates and notations can be added to provide more information. You might be particularly interested in information about careers or educational level. You may want to trace immigration patterns in the family or instead concentrate on more subjective views of people's personalities or artistic or musical talents, or involvement in politics. It is easy to indicate problems such as alcoholism or sexual abuse on the genogram to give insight into how these issues have influenced a family through the generations.

How can the genogram be used in a personal history interview? As the interviewer you might find it useful and revealing to chart one as you are planning the interview. Taking the teller as the focal point, chart the relationship as far back as you are able to, and then forward to the present. When chatting with the teller or other family members, you might pick up some information about the teller's background that you can quickly sketch into the genogram.

Rather than keeping sheaves of notes in front of you, a genogram can remind you at a glance not only of the names of key people in the teller's life, but also some of the issues you might want to raise. For instance, you might notice from looking at the genogram that the teller was the only girl in her generation of grandchildren, an observation that could lead to some questions about how she felt about that, and how she thinks it affected the way she was brought up. Or the genogram might show you a pattern of divorce going back several generations, but that your teller has been married for over 50 years to the same person. Again, that would invite some questions that you might not otherwise have asked: Why does he think his marriage has lasted, when so many others in his family did not?

Diana's experience is an example of how a genogram can work. Diana decided to do an interview with her parents, Emily and Sam, after she realized how little she and her children really knew about her parents' lives. When Diana drew her genogram, some patterns emerged that surprised her.

Like a kaleidoscope, the many pieces that make up the teller's life will fall into a unique pattern.

145

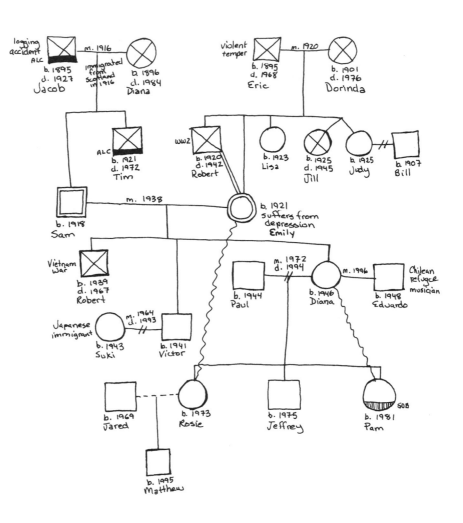

Diana's mother, Emily, came from quite a large family: she had an older brother and three younger sisters. Emily had never talked much about her father, but when Diana asked her more directly, Emily said that her father was emotionally and verbally abusive to her mother and his children. Emily was particularly close to her eldest brother Robert, who tried to protect her from her father's temper, and she was absolutely devastated when Robert was killed in World War II. For Diana, this story helped her to understand a severe long-term depression her mother went through when her oldest son, Diana's brother, also named Robert, was killed in Vietnam.

A major family secret emerged from the genogram as well. Emily had never talked about the fact that her mother, Diana's grandmother, had been pregnant when she married. Diana realized from the date of her grandparents' marriage and the date of her uncle Robert's birth that her grandparents had "had" to get married. When Diana asked her mother about it she learned that Emily and all of her siblings had known about the out of wedlock pregnancy. When their father's temper exploded, as it often did, he would remind them all that he had never wanted to get married in the first place. This resulted in Emily conveying to her own children and grandchildren her conviction that sex outside of marriage was absolutely taboo. Diana also realized where her mother's seemingly unreasonable anger came from when Rosie, Diana's oldest daughter and Emily's favorite grandchild, had a child with a man with whom she had a common-law relationship. Diana looked at the marriages in the family and the divorces, including her own, and thought about the historical events and migrations that had shaped the lives of people in her family. Although the focus of the interviews was on her parents, drawing the genogram and asking the questions about stories that arose from it gave Diana insights into her own attitudes and relationships with her children. It also gave her a feeling of being part of a fascinating ancestral chain, linked by wonderful, imperfect human beings.

There was also a pattern of alcoholism in the family. Sam's father was a logger who died when Sam was only nine. This left Sam's mother to raise two boys on her own in a boarding home where she had paying guests. When Diana asked more about the circumstances of her grandfather's death, it became clear that alcohol was a contributing factor. Sam's younger brother, Tim, was also known as a guy who liked to party, which Diana now understood as having a propensity to drink. Tim seemed unable to hold down a job, and died quite young, at the age of 51. It helped Diana to see why her fa-

147

ther was a teetotaler, and why he was so critical of his brother and his own children when they started to experiment with drinking in their teen years. It also made her wonder whether her daughter Pam's experimenting with drugs was a rebellion against the messages that had been passed down the generations about substance abuse.

Constructing a genogram is an enjoyable and simple way to gain deeper understanding of how your family works. Feel free to adapt the symbols to suit your interests and the unique characteristics of the people in your family; there is no perfectly right or wrong way of doing this as it is entirely for your own use. It might be done either by the interviewer or the teller in preparation for the recorded interview, and can be as detailed or as simple as you wish. Patterns of behavior and ways of relating and dealing with issues are often illuminated in a multi-generational genogram. Whether it reveals patterns that you like or ones you want to change is up to you.

New technology for preserving and tracing family history

A. DATA BASES

Before personal computers were common, the key to success for genealogists was organization. Large amounts of information had to be collected and kept in some kind of order, in binders or files. Data bases have made that job much easier. People now can choose from among many programs, the most widely used of which are Personal Ancestry File (PAF, used by the Mormon Church for their vast family history files), Brother's Keeper, Roots, Family Tree Maker, and Family Scrapbook. There is a common language among these data bases, so files from any of them can be put on a disk and sent to someone with different software packages. And the good data bases have, in addition to space to insert names and dates, sections for stories, notes, facts, or physical descriptions of people.

One of the miracles of computers is how fast they can organize and reorganize information. In an instant, information can shift from pedigree charts to family groups. This means that the genealogical researcher in the family can easily isolate different branches of the family if the chart is being sent out to distant family members for more information.

New technology is developing at a rapid rate; it is already possible in many cases to scan photographs into the text, and insert audio or video tape clips from the interview. This raises exciting possibilities for a multi-media approach to family history, combining family stories and genealogical research.

B. INTERNET

The search for information, stories, and names for the family tree has been revolutionized by the proliferation of genealogical websites on the Internet. The sites range from personal family websites to genealogical societies and commercial sites. There are over 13,000 websites devoted to genealogy. One website alone features over 16,800 links organized into over 60 categories! How can one possibly make use of such an abundance of information? And how can you find your own family stories in cyberspace?

Here's a lovely story, from a 72-year-old Jewish woman who was researching the history of her mother's family, named Zellermayer. "Last winter, I was reading some of my parents' correspondence, and came across a letter to them dated 1921 from a David Zellermayer in Berlin. He signed himself as a cousin, but I had never heard of him. Then there was another letter in 1957 from a D. Zellermayer in Israel, in which he tells all about himself, including names of his three children and seven grandchildren. So I posted a message on an Internet newsgroup "soc.genealogy.jewish," asking whether anyone knew anything about this David Zellermayer. Promptly I got two e-mails from people in Israel who had looked in telephone books. All in all, I got 13 addresses, so I wrote letters to all those Zellermayers, asking if they were related to David. Two weeks later, I got a fax from some-

Both men and women are most likely to search their ancestral past looking for a role model when they contemplate some arena of life for which they feel their family has left them ill--or unequipped, or when they are actually on the verge of some major rite of passage, often relating to marriage or work.

—Elizabeth Stone

149

one who could identify the David Zellermayer I was looking for. He wrote that that very afternoon he was going to the bar mitzvah of a boy who was the great-grandson of the original David. And he included the phone number. So I just dialed the number, and was able to congratulate a very stunned 13-year-old boy. Through further correspondence, we have been able to share stories about our common relatives, and fill in blanks in the genealogy."

There are people who claim to have no interest at all in genealogy. But it happens frequently that the birth of a child, the death of a parent, or the inescapable fact of one's own aging will jog an awareness of the life cycle, and that in turn will spark an interest in knowing more about one's roots. The story of each family is unique and special, no matter whether we find heroes or villains, common folk or nobility, strong characters or people with all too human frailties lurking in our family's past. We have a need to know where we come from, to give us a sense of connection with the past and a path to the future. Genealogy and family stories together give us that history.

Excerpts from Some Interviews

My father! I never thought of him in this way but then, who really knows his father, or his mother? In our dramas they play older, supporting roles, and we are always centre stage, in the limelight.
—ROBERTSON DAVIES

Interview between a 65-year-old man (H.P.) and his daughter

Interviewer: Can you start by talking about your grandparents?

H.P.: My grandfather was a butcher in a small town in southern Italy. A beautiful mountain village. Walled. He left the town on a trip to one of the bigger towns, I believe it was in the same province. And he saw electric light bulbs for the first time. When he came back, he told his friends that he had seen the fire that gave light, but you couldn't light your pipe on it. His friends just didn't believe him. They said, "Oh you think we're fools, you know, but we're not that far back in the sticks. We know there's no such thing." He died relatively early, quite soon after my father was born. I believe my father was five or six when his father died.

I: What did he die of?

H.P.: He died suddenly at the kitchen table when they were eating a meal. I've never heard just whether it was a stroke or what. But my maternal grandmother lived till 1927, I believe.

I: What was her name?

H.P.: Sorry, I can't remember at the moment. It may come to me, and I'll shoot it out some time while we're talking. My father was the youngest of seven. There were four girls and three boys. When he was five years old he used to herd the goats through the town. If people wanted milk they'd bring a container out, and he'd milk the goat right there, and they'd pay their money for the milk.

I: He was the youngest?

H.P.: He was the youngest, yes. He had four sisters and two brothers. Leonardo was the oldest brother. I know more about the brothers than I do the sisters, because they were more together, and of course, the one brother I knew quite well. There was Leonardo, Bruno, and my father. They came to North America about 1903. My dad was born in 1888. He landed in Pittsburgh with a potato bag tag on his shirt saying Pittsburgh, Pennsylvania. From there he went to a small mining town. I've tried to find since where it was. Nobody knows.

I: Do you know anything about the time when he was a little boy?

H.P.: He went to school for only two years, but he didn't spend much time as a little boy, because he was in the coal mines.

I: What was life like for his family?

H.P.: The tradespeople would come to make sure you got shoes for your children. A man would come to your house, and he stayed there maybe two days. As long as it took to make the shoes. He'd eat with the family and everything. He'd make shoes for everybody in the family. There was a story about one shoemaker who stayed with the family for a few days. And the food they ate was so hot, hot off the stove and hot with spices, that he left the house, waving his hand in front of his mouth to cool it off. It was that hot. You'd have to eat fast in that family because there were so many kids there, they'd eat it before you.

I: Was it common for kids then to only have a couple of years of school?

H.P.: It was common, yes. They didn't need a lot of school. Particularly in the small towns. He worked. He went down to the seashore in the winter, picked olives and oranges.

I: When he was very young?

H.P.: Yes, that's right. And he'd go down with his oldest sisters. I don't remember him mentioning his brother, but his older sisters, some were already married, he'd go down with them to pick. They lived in these common huts for the winter. They were migrant workers, is what they were.

I: Did he ever mention his sisters much? What kind of relationship did he have with them?

H.P.: Pretty good. The three boys, when they came here, the first money they made all went back to build their sisters' dowries.

I: What about your grandmother?

H.P.: She was pretty strong. Very little, very little, about four foot seven, I think. And her husband was six foot two. She was a tough little bird, though, a very strong woman. She ruled the roost, and when she said something, they all said yes. She raised that family and they all had good characters, you know, strong characters. They were strong people, the women more than the men. The women were real liberated women, if you want to use that term.

I: What do you mean when you say that?

H.P.: Well, they were really the driving forces in their families once they married. They could have made their husbands change their names to theirs rather than the other way around. Because they were the driving force.

I: That's an interesting perspective for me to hear many generations later, because I've kept my own name. Did the daughters stay in Italy?

H.P.: No, one went to South America, one went to São Paulo, Brazil. She has an interesting little story of her own.

153

Excerpts from Some Interviews

Our family immigrated from Finland when I was 5, my sister 7. We lived on a farm here, and I remember our first years as golden. But my sister remembers poverty, deprivation, not being able to speak English. The difference in our memories is due partly to our different personalities, and partly to the fact that she was older, understood more of our circumstances, and started school as a foreigner.

—GN

Try to end on a positive note, leaving the teller feeling good about the experience.

I: What's her story?

H.P.: Well, her story is, she and her husband got a piece of land just outside of São Paulo, which was then out in the bush. But São Paulo, as you know, has grown to over ten million people. So their land has become prime downtown land. Well, they didn't sell it, apparently. They took positions in the building. And my generation, to my knowledge, has never done a day's work, because they live off the rents. But a very tragic thing, her husband and his brother had a warehouse for the produce that they were growing. They had a bookkeeper they suspected was stealing. So they stole up one night, hid themselves, and waited for him to come back to the warehouse. The brother had a gun. When the bookkeeper came in, he tried to get away, and the brother shot him. And killed him. The brother gives the gun to my uncle, he says, "You take responsibility, because I have more education, I know more people, and I'll get you off." He didn't get him off, so my uncle spent twenty years in jail for a crime he didn't commit. My aunt raised their children.

I: Is she still alive?

H.P.: No. She was the eldest of the girls, but she died some years ago. I remember her passing. As a matter of fact, when I think about it I remember most about her passing.

I: Why do you remember that?

H.P.: I remember the letter from South America. A letter coming from South America was quite a thing.

I: So what do you remember about that time?

H.P.: My dad was very upset. He hadn't seen her in years. It was his last sister. He was quite close even though he never saw her that much.

I: So you remember a lot of sadness from him.

H.P.: Yes, there were strong family ties. I have to tell you a little about the history of southern Italy. After the war, southern Italy was a forgotten part of Italy. The government didn't care about it, the courts didn't care about it. So the only people you could trust was your family. So we had real strong—extraordinarily strong—family ties. It's almost a joke, the Italian family. Once you're accepted in a southern Italian family, you're accepted. Like your mom, my wife, she was Scottish. At first they said, "Be careful, be careful." But once she was part of our family, she was in. She couldn't make any mistakes as far as my family was concerned. So that's just a background to some of the feelings.

I: Your father, my grandfather, arrived in Pennsylvania when he was 15. His brothers were already there?

H.P.:   Yes, and they had jobs in a coal mine. But they moved from one coal mining area to another. I'll tell you one story. Their friends would carry their belongings to wherever they were going. They'd get hijacked from time to time by the Black Hand, an underworld group. So what they did eventually, was the man who was moving and a few of his friends walked down the pathway carrying his belongings, everything in one chest. His friends would walk alongside in the bush, carrying revolvers, and if they got hijacked, the friends would jump out of the bush and hijack the hijackers.

I: What kind of relationship did the three brothers have?

H.P.:   They were just one unit. That's the only way to describe it. They worked together, nobody ever said who belonged to what or what belonged to who. That's the way the relationship was, and nobody seems to have worried about it.

I: Did your father tell you a lot of stories?

H.P.:   Whatever came up, he had a story that I found interesting. I would bait him.

I: What did you tease him about?

H.P.:   I used to call him warmonger, you know. He didn't like that. He was very proud of his military career.

I: And you were a bit of a pacifist?

H.P.:   Oh I was, yes. I was half kidding and half serious.

155

One session shouldn't last more than an hour and a half or two hours.

When making a transcript, use a copy rather than the original.

I: What kind of guy was he then?

H.P.: Then? I think cock of the walk. This thing is getting too long. I'm talking too much, I guess.

I: Oh no, no. It just takes a long time. The more stories you tell, the better. It just takes a long time to get where we want to go. You said he was kind of cocky?

H.P.: I think he was.

I: Why do you think that?

H.P.: Just by looking at photos, very mafioso.

I: How did he meet your mother?

H.P.: Well, he went back to Italy several times. Remember the story I told you about his father coming back, talking about the flameless light that he'd seen? My father went back and he'd seen an airplane. He'd seen a man fly an airplane. So he went back and said, "People are flying." The people in the village said, "You're just like your father, you're a fool."

I: So tell me about meeting my grandmother.

H.P.: I think he met her through her mother, who had a store, and a place where men went to drink. She came to bring something to her mother. I think that's what it was.

I: How old was he then?

H.P.: He was nine years older, he was 24.

I: Was it love at first sight, or what do you remember hearing about that?

H.P.: Well, I can't honestly remember. He must have remembered her because he came back to her place. She'd been wooed by a lot of men. They used to sing under her window in the night.

I: What's the earliest you know about her people?

H.P.: Not very much. Her maternal grandmother was a tremendous influence on my mother, because my grandfather ran a mule train in the town down to the sea and they carried produce both ways. My grandmother ran a little store, as I said earlier. So my mother was raised to a great degree by her grandmother who was a tremendous influence on her. The grandmother, from the stories I've heard, was a very liberated woman for her time. My mother never, never went ten sentences without mentioning her grandmother and what her grandmother said. She was just a clever, a naturally clever woman.

I: What about her family, her brothers and sisters?

H.P.:   Her brothers in the late 1800s could read and write, which was not too common, in the small towns anyway. They read the Old Testament, and they said, well, this is the way God meant us to live. So they went into the bush and formed—in the 1960s it would have been called a commune, a hippy commune. They let their hair grow, they took biblical Old Testament names. And marriages were between a man, a woman, and God, and no priest was there. They just made vows between the two of them, which they made up and said under a tree, under a specific tree, I think. They were quite successful. They farmed. They tried to live the good life. Good in terms of morality.

I: What do you remember about your grandfather?

H.P.:   When he ate an apple, it wasn't just that he ate an apple, it was a ritual, it was a ceremony. He'd take the apple and he'd polish it, and he'd look at it from all the angles. Then he would take a knife, and he would peel it so very carefully and cut it in sections, and cut the core out. If there was a child near him, the child got the first slice, and it was just like eating ambrosia. It was certainly a special treat.

Another thing about my grandfather. When I was getting married, he called me downstairs, and he handed me an envelope, and he said, "This is for you to buy a new car. I could have waited until I died and left you this money in my will, but you need a new car, and you need it now. And I want to see you enjoy the car, and now that I'm living I'll see you enjoying the car. When I come to your place you can buy me a glass of wine, and we'll just enjoy each other's company." In the envelope was a thousand dollars.

157

*Interview between a 70-year-old
woman (A.B.) and her niece*

Interviewer: At what point did you decide you wanted to be a teacher?

A.B.: I think I never had any other dream from the day I started school. They had to drag me in kicking and screaming, but I came out saying I was going to be a teacher. But then there wasn't much choice in those days. You could either get married, or you could be a nurse, or a teacher, and that was about it. There were no other vocations for girls.

I: Did you find it hard to leave your family when you left to go to high school?

A.B.: I was homesick, yes. It was always wonderful to go back home. I wasn't too far away, of course. I was only 10, 15 miles away. I worked for my board for two years until I finished my grade 11. There was no grade 12 there, so I had to go to Yorkton and worked for my board there. I was too young to go to teacher's college, so I took my grade 12.

I: How did you earn your room and board?

A.B.: Washed dishes, scrubbed floors, looked after children, that kind of thing. I didn't have any time to socialize. I'm pretty much of a loner yet, but I just never had any time to socialize. In grade 12 I remember I looked after three children after school.

I: When you say you were a loner, what exactly do you mean? And where do you think that came from?

A.B.: Somehow, because I had to be alone so much of the time, I got all my satisfaction from the out of doors. That's where I went whenever I was unhappy, I'd go for a walk. When we were little, my sister and I were close, but when I went to school and she got married—she married young—well, we were apart. I think really I've always been a loner.

I: Did you have a sense of whether your family did all right financially, or were there good years and bad years?

A.B.: I know there were bad years. No clothes, you know. I can remember riding the streetcar to normal school where I did my
teacher training, and then to save money, I decided to walk. I
wore the soles right off my shoes. I can remember I met a Moun-
tie, and they were having this big ball, and I was invited to go.
And a friend of mine and I wanted so badly to go, but I had no
dress, nothing to wear. I wrote to my mother and said I just had to
have a dress. Well, she had no money to buy material, you know.
She did manufacture something, but I looked at it, and I knew I
couldn't wear it. I was just devastated. And I don't remember her
name, but this friend said, "Why are you looking so sad?" and I
told her, and she said, "Well, I've got a sister who has lots of
dresses, and I'm sure one would fit you. I'll write to her." Sure
enough, she sent me a black dress. I went to the ball, feeling like a
queen.

I: What was your first job as a teacher?

A.B.: I taught in a two-room school, and I had grades one to three,
and boarded with a farmer across the street. One narrow little
bedroom, with a curtain for a door, and when I had a bath in
there, the children tried to peek around, to watch me having a
bath. But it was beautiful country, and again, I would go for walks
in the country. I had a boyfriend there, too, but you know, it
never was going to amount to anything, because I had dreams far
beyond living in a little sod shack up there.

I: What were those dreams?

A.B.: I just wanted to travel, I wanted to see the world. I wanted to
travel more than anything. All the faraway places. I wanted to go
to a ballet, and things like that. Music. I wanted something more.
I didn't even know what there was out there. We had no radio. We
were the last people to get a radio at home, we had no telephone.
I had nothing but the outdoors, and books to base my dreams on.

I: So you saw teaching just as a way of earning some money, and
then …

A.B.: It was the only thing available for girls, either that or going into nursing. There was nothing else at the time. It was right in the Depression, you know. There was just nothing else I could do, except get married. I wasn't ready to get married. I never dreamed about marriage, really.

I: Why do you think that was?

A.B.: I wanted something better than to be a farmer's wife. I didn't want to do that. If I got married and had kids, I would be stuck on the farm, and that wasn't what I wanted. My sister loved it.

I: How old were you when you had your first teaching job?

A.B.: I was, I guess, just 18.

I: That's pretty young for being responsible for a bunch of kids and living on your own.

A.B.: Yes, and really, the normal school didn't prepare you for teaching.

I: In what way?

A.B.: Well, it was more book learning, you know, and nothing about classroom management and all that.

I: So what kind of classroom management situations would come up when you had your first job, and how did you handle them?

A.B.: Oh, dear! The only thing I can remember is that lice were going around in kids' heads. Anyway, I saw something in a child's hair, and I thought, "That's a louse," and I sent a note home. This was one of the leading families in the little town, and they were highly incensed. *Their* kid didn't have lice. I just feel that I didn't do a very good job of teaching that first year.

I: Where did you go after that?

A.B.: Mom came home one day, and she said they badly wanted a teacher up in the homestead country where my family had lived when I was a young child, and would I go. I sort of thought, well, that would be kind of nice, you know. So I said "Okay." Little did I know what I was getting into. I packed up my books and my paints, because I was painting by then. Mom drove me up. It was

a gorgeous day, I remember, a beautiful Indian summer day. I was supposed to stay in the teacherage.

So I went up, and opened the door. There was a Toronto couch. I don't know if you know what that is, but, well, it's an invention of the devil! There was a handmade table with benches nailed to it, you know, and you sat on a bench around the table. A rough wooden table, rough wooden cupboards on the wall for dishes. No stove, but an airtight heater. Do you know what an airtight heater is? They burn you one minute, and you're cold the next. And wallpaper. Blue felty kind of wallpaper that hung in loops down, you know. The teacher who'd been there before had taken up her linoleum. There was an inch-deep ridge of dirt all round the edge. Well, I just about died.

I was so homesick that I slept rigidly in my bed, and I woke up in the morning hurting, just literally hurting from the tension. They did bring me a stove. Somebody had bought a new stove, and they brought me their old cookstove, with the grate burned out, so I couldn't use the oven. But anyway I had a stove. So I made my bed. I had taken some of my pictures, and I put them on the wall. I unpacked my dishes, and I scrubbed the floor.

This was a Sunday, and early the next day on Monday I prepared for the children. I went over to the school. It was awful. Just a few old moth-eaten books, nothing in the school. Desks nailed to the floor. Then the children came. Some of these people had come up from the South, they were dried out down there. One girl, she was in grade eight or nine, she was big, and she was tough, and you didn't dare touch any of her brothers or sisters, you know. There were some Ukrainian people, not much clothing, and no books. I was so frightened, I just froze. For one week I hardly knew what my name was, I was that tight.

The road ended at my school, there was no phone, no radio. I couldn't see a light anywhere at night. I was completely surrounded by trees and completely isolated. The first week, I just

I know we have a tape of my grandmother talking, but I haven't seen it for years. I'm afraid it's lost in the clutter.

—KW

161

thought I'd die. And then the colors of the trees started to change, and they were so beautiful. And the kids, you know, they were just great. Nearly every day somebody would bring me a carrot, or a turnip, or something like that, you know. I knew that I couldn't teach too much, but if I could just bring a little bit of excitement into their lives, I felt that I would be doing a good job. Teach them the basics—arithmetic, reading, and spelling, and handwriting, and forget about the history, and the social studies. But try to make life really happy, and give them a bit of enrichment. Because I didn't think I would be staying there very long.

Every day after school I'd walk through those beautiful, beautiful woods. The white poplars with their leaves. Then come home, lock my door, have my supper, and then I wrote letters to everybody, and I got more letters then than I've ever done. Then the snow came. It was just like a fairyland. I just gloried in the outdoors there. I went for a walk every day after school, and then came home before it got dark, and locked the door. I was happy. I was really happy. It was a marvelous experience.

I: Did you still have dreams to travel and see the world?

A.B.: Oh, I never, never ever lost those. Incidentally, I have done a lot of travelling. But after I got married, with my husband. Yes, I've achieved that.

I: How old were you when you married?

A.B.: We were both 33, I think. I had lived a lot, and I was ready to get married. I wanted a family. I realized that we had a great deal in common. And that he was very much like my dad. He was quiet. I just felt that it was right, the time was right for us, and that we would make a go of it. I can't say that I was madly in love or anything.

I: Sometimes just feeling really comfortable with someone is a better foundation for marriage.

A.B.: I felt comfortable with him and he felt comfortable with me. We had the same dreams. I think I had more dreams than he had.

He was in the war, he had lived in more difficult situations than I had. I was the driving force in the marriage, because I knew where I wanted to go. He would go with me. We had a really good marriage.

(Later)

I: And now you have another move ahead of you.

A.B.: Yes, now I'm going to a seniors' place. I was booked to go on a cruise on the Danube last May, did I tell you? All ready to go, and the day before I was to leave, I had a stroke. I had to cancel. A mild stroke, but I couldn't fly. That was a bitter disappointment. The Danube, of all places not to be able to go. That was just a year ago. Then I booked to go on a cruise up to Alaska in the last week of June, and on the third night out I had a fall. I went to the bathroom, and the ship moved. It was a tiny little bathroom, and I lost my balance and reached to support myself, and there was only the curtain. I went from a standing position to a sitting position on my back, and I'm still suffering from that.

I: Are you reconciled to leaving your house here?

A.B.: At first, when my daughter suggested I go live in a seniors' place in the town where she lives, I just couldn't. The thought of leaving my house was too hard. On a day like this, when the sun comes in, the golden light in here just thrills me. I'm an outdoors person, and I love light and I love the trees and I love the flowers. So I told my daughter I wouldn't move. She was so very silent, you know. But I didn't think anything of it. Then when I went over to visit her after my fall she said, "Mom, I think you should move over here, because I can't always come when you need me." Then, of course, I had to think about it. I shed tears, I can tell you. But she took me out, and I looked at two places, and I said I couldn't live in them. I knew I couldn't. I've had enough of living in dull, dumpy places in my life. Then I looked at this other place, and when I walked in, it seemed to say, "Welcome!" So the tears dried up and I began to think, well, I guess maybe I could.

Unfortunately I didn't know Janet before she died. But being able to listen to the tape of her talking about her life made me feel as if I'd known her, and I'm sure the service I performed was more meaningful as a result.

—Anglican Minister

163

I: Looking ahead, I'm curious what you want for your grandchildren. What kind of world do you want for them?

A.B.: Oh, God! A world that is safe. A world where we save our trees and our environment. I think most of all we have to be thinking about the environment. And a world that will have no more wars. I don't like the idea of many rich people and many poor people. I would hope we could have a kind of government that would see that this wouldn't happen any more. When you think of people with billions of dollars, for what purpose when there are people sleeping on the streets?

I: What are some of the things you are looking forward to when you move?

A.B.: Well, I want to start my painting again. I used to do oils for a long time, and the last four or five years I got into watercolors. I haven't done any for a while, it's been one thing after another. But I'm going to start as soon as I get organized there.

Interview between an 80-year-old grandfather (J.T.)and his 19-year-old grandson

Interviewer: How many of you were in the family?

J.T.: There were six of us. Six children in the family. I was the youngest. Four girls, and my brother and myself, and quite a spread between us. Actually, my older sister was probably 10 or 12 when I was born. I was born in England, and father was a churchman. And we had a very comfortable home with several servants. I think there were five of them altogether, including the gardener and the gardener's boy.

I: Why did the family leave England?

J.T.: For some reason or other I never really knew, but I was told it was to do with the difficulty of educating six children, as my parents thought we should be educated in private schools in England. Part of the reason was, I think, for health reasons. A dry climate was required for my father who had tuberculosis. He wasn't supposed to live very long. Actually, he lived to 77. So he came out to Canada looking for a place. He was interested in fruit growing. And he met an English colonel who was also looking for land, who said that he'd found a beautiful place where it was very pretty, very good land, and it was going to be irrigated, and so on. Father went back with him there, and the upshot of it was that he bought property next to his land. And was on a benchland between two rivers. It had a lovely view to the north of the Rocky Mountains, with high snowy peaks and the lovely blue river, sort of a robin's egg blue in the summer time. Father, being an artist, and being quite a good artist, too, who had done a good deal of travelling around the world before he came out, fell in love with the view, and the place generally, and the western yellow pine. So we came out.

I: What do you remember about the trip?

J.T.: I was quite small, less than five years old. We came out very

I always meant to do a tape with my sons before their voices changed…but missed the opportunity. Now I just hope I make the time to do it before they leave home!

—EF

165

economically, the eight of us, and our governess, because the girls had nothing but a governess, and of course I hadn't started school yet. We landed in Quebec, and came out on a colonist train west. I think it took five days, and we slept on hard bunks, and there was a stove in the end of each car, and everybody did the cooking. Come to think of it, it must have been an amazing experience for my mother. She had been educated in Switzerland, she spoke French excellently. She'd been used to a gentlewoman's life in England, and here she was in a colonist train. I don't know whether there were even straw mattresses. I don't remember. Everything was rough and ready, and very slow. I can remember seeing whales off the starboard bow once, and I remember icebergs as we were coming into the Gulf of St. Lawrence. I don't remember much about the trip across, except I got a chocolate bar for my birthday. From there we went by stage. Our house wasn't finished. It must have been October, and we spent that winter in a boarding house.

I: Do you have any memories about that time?

J.T.: One of my important memories was about a toy. I had very few toys to play with or anything like that, and I went for a visit with my mother to the local doctor. There was the most beautiful looking red locomotive. It was a car, a coal car on the end of it, and it was about two feet long, the most beautiful thing, and I just couldn't take my eyes off it. We had tea, sort of English style. And as I walked out of the door, the doctor's wife picked it up and gave it to me. It was the most marvellous present. Even my brother and everybody wanted it. It would make a most terrific noise, and we'd roll it on the floor, get the wheels spinning, and then let it go roaring across the floor until it hit the wall on the other side. I don't know what the people downstairs thought.

I: When did you move out of the boarding house?

J.T.: In the spring. I remember seeing them planting—they planted over 800 fruit trees—and clearing land, and things like that.

I: What was your first house like?

J.T.: The house my father had built was a log place, a great big house, much too big even for the eight of us. Now, it had been built with green logs, very badly built, terribly badly built. But, of course, none of us knew that until winter came. One of my memories is sitting in the living room watching dry snow drifting across the floor in little whirls, piling up in the corner, because the house had been chinked with plaster, and the logs had shrunk, and the plaster was all loose, and wind just came right through. There was nothing to stop it. And it was cold. We were 2700 feet above sea level, so winter came fairly early, and it was sometimes 40 below. I believe it was even colder than that at times. It must have been quite desperate for my mother. We had no running water, no electric light, of course. The girls used to take hot water bottles to bed with them at night to keep them warm. Everybody did, except me and my brother. We didn't have that many hot water bottles. They would come down in the morning with a hot water bottle that was just frozen solid. And I do mean solid. I don't mean just a little ice.

I: Can you tell me about the school you went to?

J.T.: I guess I went to school in 1912. I'd be five then. The schoolhouse was down by the edge of the swamp. There were rushes and reeds. Marvelous place for ducks. Also a marvelous place for mosquitoes. The mosquitoes were terrible. They used to come up in black swarms. The school was right alongside. It was a typical little red schoolhouse, except it wasn't painted. I remember the first year there was an old man, about 70, I think, who was teaching everybody. I was one of the youngest, and there were boys and girls of 16 there. The desks were homemade, where two people sat side by side. They were just like what you read about. They had people's initials carved in them, and they were most uncomfortable. All I can remember about that first year was that when things got noisy and out of hand, this man turned us all loose out-

167

When I look into the mirror I see an elderly man, but also all my former selves at the same time.

—DJ

side. This happened about four times a day. I don't remember learning anything at all.

I: What was it like for you to be the youngest of six children?

J.T.: Well, what happened was that my brother went away, and not too long afterwards, one sister died, one twin sister, and the other one went away. And my elder sisters were not there. And so I was sort of trying to keep things together on the farm for quite some years. I used to have to get up very early to get everything done, and I'd have to get the milking done in the evening. There was endless work to do, especially cutting wood, which was the biggest chore of the lot. We didn't have machines then. It all had to be done by hand, and for years nobody knew how to sharpen a saw properly, or we didn't find them, anyway. And we did some awfully stupid things. We always got nothing but dry wood, big logs that were bone dry. Just as hard as iron, you know, been standing there for probably a hundred years, fir and tamarack. I can remember working away trying to get one round of wood off for probably an hour. Just steadily sawing. We would burn, seemed like half a cord of wood a day in the winter, and then we couldn't keep the place warm. It was very unsatisfactory. But the worst part was, that you couldn't see making any headway.

I: What do you mean by that?

J.T.: We would try to keep the fruit trees in shape. Father was good at pruning, but he wasn't able to do much work with the hoe and spade and that sort of thing. He would work and work and work trying to get a crop, and we just couldn't get it, we never did get a satisfactory fruit crop. We just saw the trees die of drought. And frost. It was quite impossible to grow fruit there because of the altitude mainly, but no one ever told us that. I was there about three years ago to sell the farm. Out of those 800 trees, there was one alive, and it was only half alive.

I: It must have been very discouraging.

J.T.: It was. The only bright thing was the fishing and the camping.

There was a surveyor who was very kind to the family, and he used to take us out camping, the whole lot of us. And he put us all in a big tepee, Indian tepee tent, a great big thing. It was about 14 feet across on the bottom, and we'd all sleep around it like this, all with our feet towards the center. He showed us how to make good comfortable beds with a log on either side and filled with fir bows so that it made it like a springy mattress, really comfortable. Those were great times, the best times of the lot, those camping trips. I remember cooking on a fire outside. Baking bread and everything.

I: I heard that when you were quite young, you'd sometimes go off for a couple of days by yourself.

J.T.: Yes, I used to get so fed up with working on the farm, and not seeing us getting anywhere. I just simply felt that I had to get away and explore. I used to go to my mother (I never remember going to my father) and just say, "I want to go away." "Well, where are you going?" "I'd like to go into the Gold Creek country." She'd say, "Well, how long are you going to be away?" and I'd say, "Oh, two or three days." "That's fine." So this was probably when I was eleven or twelve, maybe thirteen, I don't remember. I'd just take a blanket, roll up a little food in it, and an axe. I'd head off with a great deal of pleasure and anticipation. One time, after I'd made my bed and cooked my supper, I lay down and started to go to sleep, and then I heard a most dreadful noise, sort of a wailing cry. I was just scared stiff, and I scrambled up, and threw everything I had on the fire. I moved my bed between the fire and the creek, and I stayed awake for a long time. I didn't hear anything more. I was never actually sure what it was, but people tell me it was a cougar.

I: Did you tell your mother when you got home?

J.T.: Oh yes, oh yes.

I: Did she let you go again by yourself?

J.T.: Oh sure, she always let me go.

169

Peer interviewing is an activity for seniors with many obvious and some not so obvious benefits.

*Interview between an 80-year-old
grandmother (T.S.) and a seventh-grade girl*

Interviewer: When were you born?

T.S.: I was born in 1905. March 22nd.

I: Where were you born?

T.S.: In Syria. Homes, Syria. You wouldn't know where that is.

I: Did you like it there?

T.S.: Well, I came when I was five, but yes, I did enjoy being there. Of course things are different today.

I: Was there a school nearby?

T.S.: It was just a little kindergarten that I went to. I mean, just a one-room school.

I: Where did you live when you came here?

T.S.: I lived in Pittsburgh. I went to school in Pittsburgh, and loved it. I had very nice teachers.

I: How did you do in school?

T.S.: Fairly well. In fact, my eighth grade teacher went home with me one day to convince my mother that I should go on to college. She said she could get me a four years' scholarship, and my mother wouldn't have to pay anything. She urged and urged, and my mother said it's up to her. But I didn't have brains enough to take advantage of such a wonderful opportunity. I had had her for three years.

I: Was she one of your favorite teachers?

T.S.: I think looking back I remember her more than any other teacher.

I: Do you think the school system was better then than it is now?

T.S.: Yes, I do. I think the school system was much better, and I think the teachers were more dedicated.

I: Like now, some of the kids don't take school as seriously.

T.S.: I personally think, if you want my personal opinion, I think it goes with the dress code. I think that if teachers and students

dressed properly, that children would take more interest in schools. So I do think that it starts with that. I mean, we wouldn't dare go to school just in dungarees. And I remember when my boys were old enough to go to junior high—I have three sons. And the oldest boy always wanted to roll his trousers up. The boys had started this business of rolling their pants up. And I said, "Roll them down." He said "Oh Mom, all the boys do it." I said "Not you!" But today, they go anyway. Even the teachers aren't properly dressed.

I: What are your sons' names?

T.S.:   Russell is my eldest son, and George is my second boy, and Ted is my youngest boy. They all went through the schools in Belmont. We've been in Belmont for 54 years.

I: Did they fight a lot?

T.S.:   Once in a while. Not very often. They were close enough in age so that they got along fairly well.

I: Do you think you raised them up the same way your parents raised you up?

T.S.:   More or less. I was very strict with them. I wanted to know where they were, who they were going with, and I always told them they were free to bring their friends home. I wanted to meet their friends. And they were welcome to come. I didn't have that privilege. My mother didn't have the patience. My father died when I was two months old, and so she had the full responsibility of three girls. Therefore, she was against boys, and I couldn't have boys come to the house. So, as a result, when my children were old enough to have friends, I said any girls you go out with, I'd like to meet them. Bring them home.

I: Were you very close to your children?

T.S.:   Yes. We still are. My boys married three wonderful girls, and I couldn't love them any more if they were my own daughters.

I: Do you have any grandchildren?

T.S.:   I have 12 grandchildren (laugh). And six of them are married

and I have four great-grandchildren. We're still a very close family. I believe that's what keeps them all happy. We have big family gatherings at every opportunity.

I: Now there are small families.

T.S.: Yes, it's too bad. But they can still be very close if they are small families. They can be warm and loving. That's very important.

I: Yeah!

T.S.: And communication between members of the families is very important. People don't stop to explain why they do this, or why they don't do it. There's a lack of communication today.

I: Were you and your mother able to communicate like that?

T.S.: (pause) Not too much. She was busy working. And so I didn't see her much. And of course I didn't have a father. But my sisters—my oldest sister was very nice. She took care of me, combed my hair.

I: Like a mother.

T.S.: Yes, she was like a mother to me.

I: What did you and your family do for entertainment?

T.S.: As I said a few minutes ago, I couldn't bring any friends home. So I went to school, came home. To help the girls in the neighborhood, I'd put their hair up in curlers. My hair was naturally curly, so I never had to do anything with mine. But they'd crowd around me every Saturday night. I'd roll their hair up in these rag curlers. And they were happy the next morning. They'd look beautiful going to church.

I: Did you babysit?

T.S.: No, they didn't do that in my day. Mothers stayed home with their children. I did the same thing. I seldom had babysitters come so I could go out to a show, or anything like that. When there was an office party that my husband and I had to go to, my sister-in-law would come down and stay with the children. I felt that if there was ever a fire, God forbid, a young babysitter wouldn't stop to rescue three. She might pick one up on the way

out. But to rescue three boys was too much. And that was always my fear.

I: Did you have any brothers?

T.S.: No, I had two sisters older than myself. One died three years ago, and the other died three or four years ago. They both lived in Pittsburgh.

I: Did you get to visit them?

T.S.: Yes, once in a while. When my children were old enough to travel, I'd take them to visit my mother and my sisters.

I: If there was one moment in your life that you'd like to relive, what would it be?

T.S.: Well, let me see, I think all my moments were very, very happy ones. I don't know that I can answer that question, without a great deal of thought.

I: You don't have to, it's OK. So when you were 13, you had a happy childhood.

T.S.: As happy as possible under the circumstances. If I had had a brother, or my father was alive, I probably would have been happier. I worked part time after school when I was 13. That's what we did in those days.

I: What did you do?

T.S.: I worked in Woolworth's five and ten. About the only job I could get. I had to help. My mother had responsibilities. For that reason, she wouldn't allow me to date because the responsibility of raising three girls weighed very heavily with her.

I: Do you think your mother was under a lot of pressure?

T.S.: Well, it's always hard to raise three girls alone. It is today. But she did very well, we were well fed, we were well clothed. She never wanted anyone to say that because we didn't have a father we couldn't wear nice clothes. So we were always well dressed.

I: During the Depression, was your family affected?

T.S.: I think I was married by then, happily. The Depression was very hard on many people. My husband was in the insurance

173

business. And I remember one day, a woman coming begging him to allow her to borrow on her insurance so she could feed her family. And he said, yes, by all means. And she came in and he filled out the papers for her so she could get a loan on her policies. And as she was leaving, she said, "Mr. H—, I'll never forget this. I didn't know where to turn, what to use for money to feed my family. As soon as my husband starts working again, this will be paid off." There were many people in those circumstances.

I: Could you tell that the Depression was coming before it really happened?

T.S.: Yes, I think most people had some idea that something was going to happen. But there was nothing that we could do about it. The banks closed, and it came suddenly. There were a few people who were in the market and had an inkling of it. There was a very good friend of ours who had cashed some checks and was able to give some of his friends and neighbors a little money to spend, because if you didn't have money in your pocket, you had nothing Friday night. It was very hard on them.

I: Do you think there were any good things about living in the Depression?

T.S.: Yes, for our day. It helped us to be very economical, very careful, we didn't go out and splurge on anything because we remembered having no money. And I remember one of my granddaughters, I was talking to her the other day, and I said, "You young people spend so much money, and such high prices," and she said, "Well Grandma, we didn't live through a Depression." We tried to train them, but I don't think it helped much in many places. Do your parents talk much about the Depression?

I: No, but they say, "Be careful about your money." Now when we get money, we go out and buy candy and all these little things, but that probably made a big change in your life. It probably made you realize what you had.

T.S.: Well, ordinary people suffered terribly in the Depression. And those who did, have a lot of respect for money. (pause) What else can I add?

I: Did you like the presidents that were elected then?

T.S.: You mean now?

I: Were you always for the government? Or did you ever go against it?

T.S.: Oh no, we were always for the government. I was disgusted with some of the politicians who have not shown honesty. And I think it's too bad. And I think a lot of the trouble that the young people get into is because they have seen these men go into high office. And then, in your time, even, they have been taken to task for stealing, or manipulating, and so forth. And you try to respect them. But you can't when they do these things.

I: When you were raising your children, what was the neighborhood like?

T.S.: We have lived in the same house now for 50 years. We had a very nice neighborhood. We were surrounded by middle-class people. And we enjoyed our neighbors. We loved our schools. The principal of the school my boys went to always had top grade teachers. So there was no problems there. The teachers were always pleased with the way our children behaved, and we taught them to have respect for the teachers. I think children should respect their teachers.

I: What differences have you noticed between everyday life in the early days and now?

T.S.: Well, people have more money to spend now.

I: Do you think it was better now or then?

T.S.: I think we were better off then. We didn't have as much money to spend. Prices were lower, and we were satisfied. For instance, we could buy a dozen eggs for 18 cents. Today look what you have to pay. So we feel we were better off then. Now when I see my granddaughters buying shoes for their children, the prices that they have to pay! And we feel that they brought it on themselves by being ready to spend that price. So, we were better off, I think.

175

Excerpts from Some Interviews

I can't tell you how glad I am that Sid made a tape with you before he died. I know he enjoyed the process of doing it, and it is a great comfort to me to hear his dear voice.

—CR

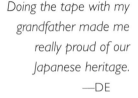

Doing the tape with my grandfather made me really proud of our Japanese heritage.

—DE

I: What did you really like about the 1920s?

T.S.: I got married in 1924. I was 19 years old.

I: What was your favorite thing around that time, what did you really enjoy?

T.S.: I enjoyed life. I didn't have any big ideas, or anything like that. We were happy.

I: You made the best of what you had.

T.S.: Yes.

I: Do you think the styles have changed a lot?

T.S.: They change and they go back.

I: Like the miniskirts.

T.S.: Sure. I remember just before I got married, we were wearing long dresses, and they were so graceful. Women looked very nice. Then they went into shorts. I think really short short skirts are awful, when they go up the knee or above the knee. There's nothing graceful about it. It goes in cycles.

I: What was your favorite music?

T.S.: We used to sing all the oldtime songs. We enjoyed them very much, and would sing together. Even my boys, when they were growing up, they used to. For instance in the summer we'd go away to a place at the beach. And they would gather together in the evening and sing. We did the same when we were first married. We'd have friends come in. I remember one of our friends played the piano, and we sang or we danced around. And that was very harmless entertainment. It didn't cost us anything except a little bit of refreshments. We did that very often, and our boys did the same thing. They had their friends in. I thought it was very important for parents to encourage their children to bring their friends home. I enjoyed being a parent very, very much. I loved every minute of it.

I: Do you think that *they* love *you*?

T.S.: Oh yes, they call me every day to see how I'm doing. We're very warm towards one another.

I: Some families just lose touch. They just separate and they don't call.

T.S.: We've always been a close family. I remember one of my daughters-in-law who came from a very small family. She loved the family get-togethers, and she said, "Oh Mom, please don't ever let us give this up." And I said "Well honey, it's up to you. I won't be here forever." She said "We sure will."

I: Do you like having family gatherings and stuff?

T.S.: Oh, we love having the big gatherings. Around Christmas I have a big dinner. It's usually a few days before Christmas so they can celebrate Christmas in their own homes with their children. It's always 28 or so of us who gather. Everybody helps, so I never have to go into the kitchen while they're there.

I: So it's not like you have to serve.

T.S.: It's a wonderful family life.

I: I hope my family's like that.

T.S.: I hope so too, but you know it's up to each one to do their share. And you can make your life what it is. Family gatherings are important. I think there wouldn't be so many divorces.

I: Yeah, if people communicated more.

T.S.: Absolutely. Communication is very important.

I: If they worked their problems out, and talked about it.

T.S.: You're very right.

I: Now some people live together without being married, and they don't realize that they should get married if they love a person. Not just live with them. So they can have the opportunity to be close to a family.

T.S.: Why do you suppose they do that today?

I: I don't know. Kids rush into things. They don't really think them over.

T.S.: They don't really want the responsibility of having someone to care for?

I: They don't share in each other's lives.

177

T.S.: It's just wonderful to be together, to do things together. Our children and grandchildren are all very thoughtful and considerate.

I: So like what your mother was to you, you were to your children. And they are carrying on the same traditions?

T.S.: Yes. I feel sorry for people who haven't had loving parents. And there are so many of them right now in this world. Children can be happy all the time if they have the right love from their parents. Today it's a high-stepping life, a fast-stepping life, everybody is intense. And they're so busy making money that they don't have enough time to spend with their children. Unfortunately. I'm sure you are very happy in your life?

I: Yes.

T.S.: How many are in your family?

I: Well, actually four, but then I've got a step-father, so it makes it five. And then my dad might get married again, so it might be six.

T.S.: You're all happy?

I: Yeah.

(After this the conversation shifted to questions by teller about interviewer's life.)

178

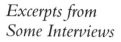

Interview between an 82-year-old
man (C.S.) and a teenage boy

Interviewer: The first question I want to ask is how you got the name "C.S." Is it short for anything?

C.S. No, it's an initial name. In the South, where I'm from, in Texas, that's the custom they had. They named their kids "J.C.", "R.H.", something like that.

I: Was that just the custom in black families?

C.S.: Yes, I think so. It was quite common in black families.

I: Tell me about the family you grew up in.

C.S.: I grew up in a family of three boys and three girls. I was the youngest. And my mother and father separated before I was old enough to know my father. And I met him first when I was around eight years old. And by not being around him, and not knowing him, I had no feeling whatsoever for him. And he lived and died in that condition. I never thought of him, I was raised by my mother and that's all I knew.

I: Why did he enter your life again when you were eight?

C.S.: My mother wanted me to see him. And I went to live with him and his new family. He had a girl and a boy. And we didn't get along, so I didn't stay very long. And I went back to my mother and never saw him again.

I: What year were you born?

C.S.: 1908.

I: And where, exactly?

C.S.: Bryant, Texas. That's 80 miles from Houston, Texas, and 130 miles from Dallas.

I: Tell me what your mother was like.

C.S.: She was the greatest!

I: Did your mother remarry, or was she a single mother with six kids?

C.S.: She was a single mother with six kids. Each one of us, as we became old enough, went out to work to help.

I: It must have been hard.

C.S.: It was rough. Very rough. And there wasn't much work to do. Only picking cotton, chopping cotton. That was the work we did. Farming was the main thing. So we went out, and we all worked. I got very little schooling, about the fifth grade. But I taught myself along the way. I can read anything, I write my own checks, I balance my checkbook, and everything, even though I had very little schooling. It was a case of "had to," not because I wanted to. Each of us had to help as he grew older. I was the baby.

I: Tell me about your memories of school.

C.S.: See, back then, you didn't go to school until you were seven years old. And by that time your mother had taught you to read and write. So I went to the fifth grade, and then I was old enough to go help Mama. I had no problems at school for the simple reason that I wasn't allowed to misbehave. I would do a lot of little things, but no big things.

I: What sorts of little things would you do?

C.S.: Slapping kids in class, and stupid things like that. You'd get to go sit in a corner by yourself for a while, till you'd repent for what you did. At that time they could spank you on the hands at school. Then they would write a note to your mother or your parents, and you had to take it home, and give it to them. And you knew what you were going to get. That was kind of rough, to have to take that note home and give it to your mother. I remember one time I hit a kid—I don't know why. And they gave me a bucket, and I had to go all along the school and pick up pebbles in the school yard. Then I had to dump them, pick them back up, put them in the bucket, take them over here and dump them. And I did that for half a day for punishment.

I: How did your mother earn money for the family?

C.S.: All she knew to do was housekeeping. And she worked for rich white people. They helped her, and they knew our condition, and we did okay.

I: What did you know about her parents?

C.S.: I knew my grandmother, and I saw my grandfather before he died. But I was very young, and I don't remember too much about him.

I: What was your grandmother like?

C.S.: She was very sweet. And my mother was the perfect picture of her.

I: I want to ask you some questions about your experience of being black in America.

C.S.: Well, here's the way that worked. You had your place. That's the way they put it. You did what you was supposed to do. You didn't do anything that you wasn't supposed to do. You were black. You did your thing and you didn't bother with the other thing. And that's the way it was. And that's the way we did it. That way, you stayed out of trouble and you lived all right. You did not even mix. We went to separate schools, black schools and white schools. And the school at that time was one big building. You went from first grade to twelfth at the same school. Not like now.

I: When you say, "You had to know your place," what exactly do you mean?

C.S.: When the bus came, you rode in the back of the bus. You did not get on the bus, and go sit up in front, because you knew that was for the white people. They had a section at the back with a sign that said "Negro." And that was the way it was, not just there, but all over the South. And that's the way it worked. If you stepped out of your place, then you were in trouble. You'd get arrested. So we were taught to do what we was supposed to do, and it was no problem, you know what I mean? You do what you know. That's what we did, that's what we had to do to get along. And you were taught to get along.

We were taught to respect all older people, no matter who they were. Not like now. If a grown person told you not to do

181

something, you didn't do it. That's the way we was raised, and that's the way the time was, then. We were brought over as slaves from Africa, and that's the way we worked it, all the way through. You worked for the man who had the money, and that was white people. There were no rich black people, not in the United States. Might have been some rich ones somewhere in the world, but not here.

I: How far back can you go in your family?

C.S.: My grandmother, that was all. I didn't know my father's folks at all.

I: What sorts of values did your mother teach you when you were growing up?

C.S.: Well, I think she did a very good job, because I've had no problem. I've never been arrested, I've never been in jail. Now I've got tickets for speeding, but that's as far as I've gone in breaking the law. And I think it was because of the way I was brought up, because you paid attention. You didn't just listen. You paid attention. And you did what you were told. Kids do what they want to do now. But then you did what you were told, or you'd be punished. It was that way.

I: Was going to church important to your mother?

C.S.: Oh yes, you had to do it. As long as you were under that roof, you did what you were told. You didn't do what you wanted to do. And Sunday, the Sabbath, you respected that day. You didn't go play, you ate your food, you went somewhere and sat down, you kept your mouth shut unless you were spoken to. If the adults had company, you went away into the yard and you stayed there. You did not run in and out of the house, yelling and slamming the door. You knew that they wouldn't allow it, and you didn't try. They taught you well. But it paid off. I grew to be a man, I stayed out of trouble, I learned to take care of myself, and now look at me! I have everything I want and I'm happy.

I: How widespread was segregation?

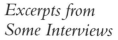

C.S.: Segregation was all over the South. And even a tiny bit in California, when I came here.

I: In what way?

C.S.: Well, here you couldn't have interracial marriage. They wouldn't marry you. When I was living in Red Bluff, a friend of mine met a Hawaiian girl and they fell in love. They had to go to Oregon to get married. So there was a bit here, but not as bad as it was in the South. You lived in one section. White people lived in another. You knew your section, and didn't try to live in the other section. You go along with the program. After I moved to California, I went to Mississippi, and there at the time, you got on the bus, paid your fare, got off the bus, and went in by the side door. Well, I didn't know that. In Texas, you had to sit separately, but you got on the bus, paid your fare, and walked back to the back.

I: So what happened to you in Mississippi?

C.S.: They called the cops. And they said, "Where are you from, boy?" And I told them I was from California. Then they told me what I was supposed to do. I said I was sorry. I didn't go way down there to get in trouble. This was 1945. Another time, I went into Michigan. We left our cars, and went on the train. We got in there about 4:00 in the morning, and saw a little coffee shop. And they wouldn't serve us. The waitress was quite young. She was embarrassed. She said, "I'm sorry, we can't serve you here." Well, we knew why, we didn't have to ask her why. So we went around to the back, and they gave us some coffee. Why get into trouble? You can't better the conditions by yourself, so why get arrested, and put in jail, and all that? You go along with the program. You may not be satisfied, but it makes it better for you.

I: Getting back to your family, when you were growing up, what sorts of things would you do together?

C.S.: Oh, we had a lovely time. It might not have been great to other people, but if you only know a certain thing, you'll enjoy doing it. So we would get together, have dinners, play games,

things like that. That's all we knew to do. We didn't realize that you were supposed to have more. You have to know about it to miss it. Well, we didn't know about it. We were born poor, we lived poor, and that's what we thought we was supposed to be. And when I came to California, and went to work, and got money in my pocket, I thought that was the greatest thing.

I: How did you come to California?

C.S.: My oldest brother came to Riverside, California. It was so nice that he told my mother that we should all move, because everything was better, it was easier to make a living. So we decided to come out in 1925. We sold our home, and moved to Red Bluff, California. The whole family, everyone came out together. And we found out that the weather there was just about the same as it was in Texas, which was very, very hot. So then, in 1929 we moved to San Jose. And I've lived here ever since. The only time I've been away is during World War II, when I worked for the Navy. Defense work. Now I'm doing good. I worked hard, I worked on the ranches, then I got a good job at Macy's department store, right here in San Jose. I retired from there, I get my pension from there. And that's pretty good for a guy with only five years of school. I don't have the certificate, but I know right from wrong. That's the way I was taught. I know that I don't abuse you, because I don't want you to abuse me. And if you practice that, you get along good. You don't go along hating the way it used to be. You get along loving the way that it is—that makes the difference. You can go along feeling sorry for yourself. And you get nowhere, exactly nowhere. You appreciate the things you have, not what you didn't get.

I have friends, and everywhere I've ever been, it's been that way. When my birthday comes on the 16th of April, the whole neighborhood comes. We put a big sign across the garage, and I barbecue two turkeys, a ham, and we all drink, and have a good time. And it's been that way since 1971 out here. I treat people

like I want to be treated. Even little kids, who don't usually care about old people. All of these kids here have grown up around me. They treat me like their grandfather. It pays off. You do the right thing, you get the right thing back.

I: You sound very happy with your life.

C.S.: That's right. When I had my heart attack, the kids in this neighborhood came to hospital. But they couldn't come into my room. So I asked the nurse if it would be all right if we took one reception room. And they gave me permission. And all the kids in the neighborhood came to the hospital, and brought ice cream and cake. And the nurses couldn't believe it. How could that many young white kids like an old black man like me? I had a good time. I've got nothing to be sorry about. Nothing.

*Interview between a 63-year-old
woman (M.F.) and her daughter*

Interviewer: Now I want to know about your parents' backgrounds. First of all your father.

M.F.: I know very little about his background. He told us very little about it. And his mother was a pretty limited person. I used to visit her about once a year. And I have to admit, I never looked forward to those visits. She lived in what I always considered sort of a squalid place, something like a bungalow. Somehow it always felt dirty there, and I think it was because Grandmother didn't do any housekeeping, and it always smelled dank. Maybe that's why I always react so violently to the smell in our cabin, incidentally. And I can't remember any real conversation with Grandmother. I might be doing her an injustice, but that's the case. The only thing that I remember is that whenever I came, I was appalled at her glasses, because they were always dirty. And I would take some hot water and soap, and wash off the glasses. And Grandmother would exclaim that the joy of seeing me made her see much better. And I always tried to tell her that it wasn't me, it was that her glasses were clean.

My father was a very quiet person, not talkative. He read the newspaper regularly and diligently, but I don't recall him ever reading a book. I'm quite sure that he was as honest as the day is long and as a salesman, I know he was very well liked.

I: Aunt Hanna once said that he didn't have the killer instinct to be a really successful salesman.

M.F.: She is older than I am, as you know, and may have seen something that I didn't see. But that's probably quite correct. He was not a person who would walk over bodies to get somewhere. I don't think he was particularly ambitious.

I: Can you give me a sketch of your mother?

M.F.: My mother, I think, was a very artistic person, a very imagina-

tive person. She herself talked about the fact that she wanted to be a writer in her teens, and was very disappointed that she couldn't be one. I think she was a sickly teenager and had to pace herself. Then eventually she entered the stream all young girls did, she became a secretary. While I knew her at home, she quite obviously fit the stereotype of a housewife. She ran the household well. She would spend a lot of time doing embroidery, handwork. But again, it was very typical for people in those days to buy a pattern and follow it. She was meticulous in her work, but it wasn't until we came to North America that she branched out, and threw patterns to the wind, and followed her own imagination. And you remember, she really produced beautiful artistic things.

I: And I think they got more creative as she got older.

M.F.: Yes, that's right. She was a very warm person. I remember that when I was growing up there was a mark on the fence. And it was made by peddlars, who had their own communication system telling other peddlars which houses were worth patronizing. And ours was quite clearly one where it was worth stopping, because you would get something to eat. What else would you like to know? Really, in retrospect, the life those women lived was pretty restricted. Every day she would go shopping. The greengrocer, baker, and butcher were all in the area. She did all the shopping for my father. He wouldn't even buy a tie for himself, or shoes. She was in charge. I know your father would crucify me if I tried to buy him shoes. But once a week on Friday, there was the coffee circle. And that was a very time-honored institution, where the same women—and they weren't feminists, by any means—perhaps seven people—would get together. You might think they would take turns meeting in each others' houses, but they always went to the same cafe in the wintertime, and a particular restaurant on the river in the summertime. I'm trying to think whether they played cards—I don't think so.

I: What did they do with their children?

187

M.F.: That's a good question! I think we were all in school. They certainly didn't bring us along. What else can I tell you about Baba? She read a lot. She went to the library, and tried to keep abreast of what was going on. She kept some books tucked away in her laundry closet, which had a lock. And one of them was on sex education. But it was always locked away. And I always knew where the key was! I don't remember whether she ever talked to me about sex. I don't think she did. I got all the information from books and my peer group, really.

(Later)

M.F.: There were large grounds with the house, a huge garden. Easter egg hunting was just a picnic! And a huge courtyard with a spreading walnut tree in the corner. I remember climbing up the walnut tree one time, and my father saw me. I was sitting very high up, and he was really petrified. That's the only time he ever hit me. He was so relieved when I came down, and upset, too, that he slapped me. First he threw his keys at me to make me come down. That was the house from which I started school.

I: Let's talk about what school was like. Did you enjoy school?

M.F.: I think really we were all apple-polishers.

I: What do you mean by that?

M.F.: Well, to wipe the blackboard was really bliss. There were some teachers who lived nearby, and I always walked home with them. I probably even carried their bags, I wouldn't have put it past me! I think kids wouldn't be caught dead doing that now, but somehow a lot of kids did it then. I don't think I was unique. It took me 10 or 15 minutes to walk to school. It wouldn't have occurred to *anyone* to drive me—well, there wasn't anything to drive, anyway! There was an old mare there, of course. Actually there was a sort of horse-drawn carriage, and my cousins would ride in it. They were much better off than we were, and the social difference was obvious, even to me at that point. I guess I felt they were a little spoilt. And a natural target to bite. And I did bite Margaret.

Margaret is a year older than I am, and I bit her because she stood in front of her garden gate, spread her arms, and said, "You can't go in, that's *my* garden!" So I bit her. What else could I do? Do you want to know what happened after I bit her? Margaret of course let out a yell, and Aunt Milly came, like a bullet, and demanded that my mother punish me. I think Mother empathized with me a little, but she felt that she had to punish me. So she told me that I was to go to my room. It was a nice day, and I really wasn't happy at being in my room. But Aunt Milly kept coming to see whether I was duly punished and humbled and penitent. And every time I heard her footsteps, I would dash to my doll carriage and start playing. And Aunt Milly was irate, because this was no punishment in her eyes.

I: Didn't you tell me that Baba was quite ill at one time?

M.F.: I don't know whether she had a tumor, but I know it resulted in a hysterectomy. I don't know whether it was cancer—I just know that everyone was very very concerned about her. This is something I recall very vividly. Mother being packed into a taxi, with a cushion behind her, and I was told that she was just going to a spa. And somehow, that was completely outside our style of living. I knew that Mother wouldn't just take off like that. And I remember I had sleepless nights—literally, I didn't sleep a wink. I couldn't have been more than six years old or so. I was worried, because I knew something was wrong, but nobody would tell me anything. It was only after she had had the operation that I was allowed to see her in the hospital. I remember it was a Catholic hospital, with nuns. And the surgeon told me that my mother was going to be okay. Well, nobody had told me before that that she was not okay. I think it was at that point that I resolved that it's always more fair to level with people. One can live with truth much more easily than with one's own fantasy.

I: Can we go back to your cousins for a minute. Didn't your two families live together?

189

M.F.: Yes. Baba and her sister were pretty close, and we more or less grew up together with our cousins. Every Sunday we would go on outings together. The destination was usually a restaurant, where we would have a glass of milk and a sandwich, and come home again. They were really a very important part of my growing up, but I didn't always get along with them. However, we grew out of it.

I: Did you celebrate Christmas together?

M.F.: No, we had Christmas just within our individual families.

I: Tell me what that was like.

M.F.: Well, I never had any part in decorating the tree. I would be called up once it was all in its glory. The decoration consisted of paper baskets, filled with nuts and candies, and candles. Aside from the baskets, there was nothing that wasn't edible on the tree. It was usually a small tree, standing on a table. I remember there was a special plate of goodies for the maid. And the presents were there. We usually had a goose dinner. That was one of the few occasions that we ate in the big dining room.

I: One of the stories I vaguely remember is of a teacher who had dinner with you and buckled the tablecloth into her garter belt. Could you tell me that story?

M.F.: Well no, it wasn't at our house. Hanna was taking French lessons privately. And this woman would come every week to give her lessons. She was as blind as a bat, and thin as a stringbean. And she was one of those people who was peripherally related to aristocracy, one of those country cousins who was tolerated and occasionally invited when they had a big do, but really not part of it. So she had to earn her living by giving French lessons. And once she was invited to a posh banquet in a mansion. And she was forever on the run, because she had to catch trains hither and yon to get to her French lessons. And this was one of those times when she was just bolting her meal, when her garter came loose. So she surreptitiously adjusted her garter under the table, and then real-

ized that she had to leave to catch the train. So she jumped up and ran. But she hadn't realized that she had caught the tablecloth in her garter. And as she ran, all the assembled guests lost the tablecloth and everything on it. But it was great, because she would tell those stories on herself. That's how we found out about it.

Another time, when we lived at the mill ... The mill was on a hill, so you could either get there by following a road, or climb a rather steep path past the garden, and it wasn't lit up at all, it was pitch black. And in wintertime when it was slippery, they would sand it a bit, because it was a shortcut from the village. And once this French teacher came very late for her class. And she was as dirty as all get-out, and bruised, and exhausted. We couldn't figure out what had happened, and she said that she had to pull herself up along the garden gate—it was a very long path—and what happened was that because she couldn't see very well, she very carefully avoided the sanded part, thinking it was the ice. And she came up on the ice. So she was really just a mess. But she always told on herself.

I: What kinds of things did you play when you were a kid?

M.F.: Well, I got my first pair of skis when I was five or six years old. There was this slope behind the mill to ski on. And I scooted down there. Buying skis is not like it is now. We would go to a guy named Seifert, and he made hickory skis—no steel edges of course. And I had a sled, and skates, and later when we moved to our own house, there was a lake nearby to skate on. When I got older, I joined a hiking club, and we'd go away for the weekend. I thought I was a terrific skier, but there were no lifts, and the slopes weren't very steep. When Dad and I went back there last year, we tried to find the slopes I skied on. I was appalled at what I thought were great hills. They were really quite small. I suppose what we did was more like ski touring.

191

Interview between 63-year-old parents and daughter

This daughter interviewed her parents individually when recording up to the time that they met and married, and then talked to them both about their life together. Interviewing two people at a time is a bit risky, but sometimes works as long as one person does not dominate the conversation. This conversation had a lot of laughter and teasing back and forth.

Interviewer: So you both immigrated to North America just before the war and came to the same university. How did you actually meet?

Mother: Do you want to hear it from me, or from Dad? Okay, well, I had some friends who knew this chap. And they told me about him, and said to me, "He's from Europe, too. You might be interested in him." And I think Dad was told exactly the same thing about me. And eventually we met at some sort of student meeting.

Father: We met at a party.

M: That's right. We met at the home of a mutual friend. And Dad walked me home. Which was very pleasant in one way, but on the other hand it was very embarrassing, because I had just moved into this place on Hazelton Street—was it Hazelton?

F: Yes.

M: I had moved only that day or the day before, and I had *completely* forgotten the apartment number. So when we got to the apartment building, I think I tried the key in various locks. I just couldn't remember where I was. Eventually the key fit. Do you want to add something to that?

F: Well, I first stayed in a boarding house and then, through my friend Johnny who was a student in my class, I got into a student co-op. So I lived in the student co-op which was not far from Hazelton Street. And then I began to associate with him and his pals, and got to know them quite well. Then I went away for the summer—that was 1942. I had various summer jobs. I first worked for a steeplejack company, then I got a job in a clothing store. But then the immigration department got after me because I had changed jobs without notifying them, or something, and they insisted I had to do agricultural work. So I did that for a while, then came back in August. When I got back, a girl I knew said to me, "You really should meet my friend." And I said "Why?" and she said, "Because she's from Europe, too." So I thought that was kind of ludicrous, but then I did meet her at this party. And we got on very well.

I: How long did you go out together before you married?

F: Well, we met in the late summer of 1942 and got married in early summer 1944. And I must say, it's not altogether clear to me when we decided to get married.

M: It was pretty clear to me.

F: Yes, I know. It was clear to Mom a lot earlier than it was clear to me, that's perfectly right.

M: That's true, it might not have been clear to you whether or when we were going to get married. It was more clear to me! We met in the fall, and at Christmas you came home with me to the farm. That's when you got your first present from me, *War and Peace*, and I don't think you have read it yet, have you?

F: Well, I've read most of it.

M: We saw each other quite frequently, because the school of social work was in the same building as the department of economics, and we shared the library. I don't think I ever went to the library as much as I did during that period. We saw each other there quite a bit. We saw each other on weekends. There were all sorts of little dances, and I remember one time there was a big dance in one of the local downtown hotels. I tried to politely find out whether he wanted to take me to that dance. And Dad wasn't really interested in that sort of thing. But a few days before the dance, Dad got a call from a chap in his class, asking for my phone number,

193

because he wanted to ask me to the dance. But before he had a chance to phone me, Dad phoned to say that he wanted to go after all, and would I go with him. I agreed, and had barely hung up when George called, and was very surprised that Dad was taking me to the dance. I think we ended up with the three of us going together.

F: It wasn't that I wasn't interested, I think I was too busy or something. And then I decided at the last minute that I didn't want George to take her to the dance, so I better take her myself. So I did.

(Later, about life in California with two small children.)

F: We moved to California from New York, because I had a job at Stanford, and that's where you started going to school. You remember that. That's where we took you to a speech therapist for your lisp, but she felt it was more important to cure you of your Bronx accent!

I: From your point of view, Dad, what was family life like at that point?

F: Well, I thought we had a very good time there. We lived in what I suppose would now be regarded as temporary student housing, but I thought it was adequate for a family with two little kids. Of course the physical surroundings were very attractive, and we went out for picnics—you may recall that—in the surrounding hills and on the beach, and south to San Jose, and all the state parks that were around. I thought it was a pretty good life. You remember, we went camping in Yosemite, both in the valley, and up in the meadows. In fact, that was the period in which we did most of our family camping. We bought the tent and camping gear in San Francisco, and we still have some of it. We went on picnics almost every weekend, and went camping when we had more time. One reason for not staying there, even if we could have, was that Mom said, "There's no change of seasons here." That somehow seemed wrong.

M: Yes, I missed the winter.

I: Mom, what was it like to raise two small children there?

M:Well, you were not quite six, and David was not quite two. I remember the trip to Stanford. We rented a U-Haul truck and put all our belongings into it. It was probably a contravention of all safety rules, but we put a mattress into the back of the station wagon, and the two of you could just play there and sleep. I think you entertained each other quite well. I remember arriving in Stanford just loaded up with clothes, because at at least two motels we stayed in, the owner of the motel just heaped second-hand clothes on us. David got a cowboy jacket that way.

You started school there. A schoolbus left from the student residence, and you, together with all the other kids would board the bus each day. David—he was an adorable little tyke then, blond curly hair, and very good-natured—started nursery school. As Dad said, we lived in sort of row housing. You lived cheek-by-jowl with your neighbors, with a common front and back yard. There were lots of kids to play with. Poor David—we didn't give him toy guns to play with, and all the other kids had toy guns and rifles. Consequently, David was in demand as the "fall guy." Whenever one kid pulled out a toy gun, David would fall down and pretend to die. Now I don't know whether I irrevocably damaged his psyche, because he could never attack them, he always had to defend himself.

F: I remember something that happened around that time. There was a favorite children's radio program, called "Big John and Sparkie." And every Saturday morning, they'd go through various routines and tell stories. This was before TV and the cartoons they have now. So it was all in the mind and the ear. One of their routines was that they'd say, "Let's see how many children have tidied up their rooms, and brushed their teeth, and so on. I see you, Judith, in Los Angeles, your room looks a bit untidy, and you, Bob, in San Jose, you need to clean up your room," and this sort of thing. And then they would have a contest to see whether the

195

boys or the girls had tidier rooms. And I think you asked us about this, and we, being rational parents, tried to explain to you that this was just make-believe, they couldn't really see through the radio. And you nodded sagely that you understood this. But then one weekend, you messed up David's room, because you wanted the girls to win. When we questioned you about it, it turned out that while you kind of believed what we said, you really weren't quite sure.

Interview between an 80-year-old woman (G.O.) and her daughter

G.O.: During the hard times, the hungry '30s, as we called it, from about 1929 to 1935, it was a very strenuous time on the farm, with poor, dried out crops. I remember seeing the fence posts with the land drifted so high it covered the fence posts, which were about 4 foot high. It just seemed awful to have the land moving like that. The farmers had to plant grass crops to hold it down.

I: Did you have enough to eat during this time?

G.O.: Oh, yes. We were on the farm so we were well off. It was in towns they weren't. On the farm we had meat, milk, eggs, and mother made cheese so we didn't have any trouble at all living. I remember one year when dad took a load of wheat to the mill in Unity which was 15 miles away and came back with 10 sacks of ground wheat flour in 100-pound sacks. It was stored upstairs so it would keep dry, and we had enough food for that year. So, we weren't hard up at all, as far as food was concerned, as the people in town. We grew most of our own vegetables and canned, and we had honey from the bee hives. I remember one day mother sat down at the table and said, "Well, the only thing we bought for this meal was tea and salt," which was quite a revelation to me. We learned how to cook with honey instead of sugar, and to can with it as well.

I: You and your sister must have had a lot of chores on the farm.

G.O.: Oh yes, we did. Dorothy was very good at cooking and doing the gardening and developing new kind of plants that we could grow in Saskatchewan because the growing season is rather short. I did more with being outside, milking the cows and I liked to ride horses, and I had my own special one.

I: What was your horse's name?

G.O.: Bud.

197

I: Did you drive any of the sort of heavy farm machinery?

G.O.: Yes, yes, I did. With horses on it. On the plough you had to have four horses, on two furrows, which meant you had to harness them all, and get them out there, and hitch them up. The horses learned how to do all this quite well. Then in harvest time, when we couldn't afford more men to work on the farm, I drove a stook team for quite a while.

I: What's that?

G.O.: Well, that is a team on a hay rack. You go around and pick up the sheaves, throw them on with a pitch fork and then drive it up to the threshing machine. Dad used to throw it off so I could sit down for a while.

I: It would have been really heavy, heavy work.

G.O.: Yes, it was. But I was strong and young so it didn't really matter. You learn how to pitch it up so it hits right on the hay rack.

I: Were there tractors?

G.O.: No, not then. We had all farm machinery for horses. It would take perhaps eight to 10 horses on a machine to go out and do the work, and of course during the summer we would have four to six men all the time because the horses had to be groomed, brushed, harnessed, fed, come home for lunch and be watered and have grain, and then go out again, and we had to take a lunch out to the men. In the afternoon we had to make something for it quickly. It was nice to see the horses going up and down the field, instead of the tractors. I feel badly that when I visited the old home farm not long ago, and the only thing alive on it was the dog. There was a big barn there, and the elevator where we kept the grain, and the chicken house, and the Royal Suite where the Clydesdales lived. It just seemed sad that they haven't … one of our relatives has the farm. Now, he's a good farmer, but he only does it with tractors and machinery, and he built a big machine shed where he puts all the machinery in the winter and works out there fixing it so it's ready for spring. He works night and day as

long as you can keep doing it in the summer. It's a different story entirely, but it doesn't seem like a farm to me when you don't have all the stock to look after and produce everything for yourself.

I: You told me last time, that you got your driver's license about that time.

G.O.: Yes, when I was 16. I just wrote to Regina, which is the capital of Saskatchewan, and asked for my driver's and sent my address and my age and my birthday, and they sent it to me.

I: No test?

G.O.: No, nothing. There was no place to have a test, so you learn how to drive quite quickly because you'd have to drive out to the men in the field to take their lunch and do other things that you wanted to do.

I: What did you drive?

G.O.: I think we first had a Chev. A '32 Chev, with gear shift of course. Nobody ever heard then about automatic transmission, that was never in our scope at all. It is a new thing. We learned how to look after it. We couldn't just put the purple gas in the car because that was for farm machinery, because it wasn't taxed you see. The gas we used in the car was taxed for the road maintenance.

I: What were you like as a teenager?

G.O.: Well, I was happy and I had a lot of friends in the district. We usually went to a lake somewhere in the summer and had a lot of picnics. I made ice cream every Sunday because we had ice blocks that Dad cut at a lake in the winter and brought home and put into the bottom of the ice house, which was maybe ten feet deep in the ground. Then we would fill it full of straw in between the layers of ice. I would go in there and find some ice with an axe and take it out, put it in a sack and hit it with the axe and chop it up so it was small and it could go into the ice cream freezer. I usually did that every Sunday. It was a nice treat.

I: This was for the family or for friends?

199

G.O.: No, for the family.

I: Did you have any boyfriends at this time?

G.O.: Yes, all of the kids that went to the high school had grown up together. If you wanted to go out, you could go out on horseback, because that is what we had. Some of the kids got old cars and we went out in those. I met my husband in Grade Eight, when we were writing our Grade Eight exams. He went to university to start a degree in science in Saskatoon when I was in home economics and then he went on to Alberta to get dentistry because it wasn't taught at Saskatchewan.

I: What did young people do when they dated?

G.O.: Well, you would usually go to a dance. We had dances in the various schools. Every Friday night was dance night. The people of the school would have to clean up afterwards, sweep the floor and whatnot so the school would be ready on Monday. I remember one old fellow who could play the accordion. He was a Norwegian, I guess, and he would come out every time and play the accordion. There was another old fellow who could play the fiddle and then you would have somebody on the piano, if it was there, so it was certainly loud enough, and there was a gas lantern in the school so we could see. No electricity of course. And then a couple of the ladies of the district would put a big copper boiler on the wood and coal stove, and make coffee in a bag in this boiler and take the bag out, and there was the whole boiler full of coffee.

I: And these were dances where people of all generations came?

G.O.: Oh yes, the parents would come and they would bring all the children because, of course, there was no babysitter. You never left the children at home, you brought them. If they got tired then they'd go to sleep on a desk and sleep through all the noise. We were supposed to always go home early, but sometimes we were a little later.

I: The teen years can be difficult years sometimes.

G.O.: They are not difficult when you are busy all the time. It's not like doing nothing all day as you can in town, and there weren't too many that could get together because they would have to come by horseback and therefore you didn't get into a great deal of difficulty. There wasn't much time to play, you had to get your work done first. The cows had to be milked night and morning, and the horses had to be fed, and we always had pigs, so all of those things had to be done before you went out to play. Dad did build a tennis court for us on one section of the farmstead. It was a terribly hard job for him to do and he wasn't very well. He did it with one of those skids that you do roads with, a team on a skid, and took the sod off and then tried to keep the space for the tennis court without grass growing on it. We did play, and a lot of the kids used to gather and play on this because this was a novelty in the country to have a tennis court. It was one way of passing your time and being happy about life.

I: I guess what I am saying is it's a time when young people look to their own future, want more independence, think about what life is going to be like, and I just was trying to get a sense of that.

G.O.: Well, we weren't really a problem to the parents as young people are now, living in towns. We had lots of work to do. I remember one night I came home at 4 o'clock in the morning. We had just stopped on the way home from the dance to talk, and mother was a little upset about that. I think of all the boys in the district and they never seemed to get into any difficulty, any trouble of any kind. Usually, of course, the farm children got married early.

I: What did you see for yourself? What kind of future did you see for yourself?

G.O.: I didn't want to stay there for a lifetime.

I: What did you want?

G.O.: Well, I wanted to do something. Mother insisted I was going to go to university, and I wanted to live in the town for a while, because I had lived on the farm all that while and it wasn't too en-

201

tertaining. I can't remember parents and children arguing or getting into any trouble, or the children being delinquent. There were never gangs or anything of that nature as we have found since, where people are living in towns. I think the closeness of living in a town causes this irritation and arguing to go on. One kid decides to do something and another one bets them, and they get into a lot of difficulties that they know very well they shouldn't. Also, for our schooling we had a lot of homework because we went to this farmhouse school where there was one teacher and all the grades of high school. Of course, you know, the lab was a disaster. We tried to do a few experiments but we'd have to read it up instead. The teachers we had were understanding and not condemning, because they knew the families, so it was well adjusted to farm life.

I: What year did you graduate?

G.O.: 1940.

I: So this is after the war had started. How did the Second World War affect your family and friends?

G.O.: Well, a lot of the young men went. My husband was in the army, but that was after we got married in '43. Because he was in the university and he was taking dentistry, they wanted him to finish that to be in the army as a dentist. It was an accelerated program. You see, we had just come through hard times where we didn't have any money, we had to make our own fun. You didn't spend a lot of money on liquor because you didn't have it. However, a lot of places made beer, and Mother knew how to make beer. It was a pleasant drink for the summer, and the workers used to have that here. She got that idea from England because that's what they did there. They always had beer in the cellar and whoever was working there would have beer to drink instead of pop or something of that nature. We didn't have pop of course.

I: You were probably better off for it too. You went to Saskatoon to university.

G.O.: I went in '35 I think it was, which was just on the edge of no money. My sister went in '34, and she was in poultry, in the field of agriculture. I had to stay home one year because we only had 600 bushels of wheat and that would be just enough to plant the crop the next spring, so I stayed home. That was the winter that Mother started to direct plays to keep us kids that couldn't go anywhere interested, and we went around to the different schools and I took a correspondence course in English which was time consuming and interesting, so we got through the winter just fine, and the next year was a bit better. I went back to Saskatoon.

I: When you were there did you board?

G.O.: No, no. We rented a little suite. My sister and I took everything we needed from the farm to eat, all except milk; we had to buy that, and bread I guess. That was the first year. Then we rented a house. A poor little house near the university and we rented it for a number of years. After we kids left university, mother and dad liked to go there in the winter. Dad would curl and meet all the people he knew there and they would meet every Saturday night and have a dinner at one of the houses, about six couples I guess and they enjoyed that. It is just like the 'Snowbirds' now. They went to Saskatoon to live for the winter and it was more exciting for them than staying on the farm.

I: And for you, living in the bigger city—it must have been very different?

G.O.: Oh, very different. I could drive the car by then. I remember driving the car down with our clothes and books and things to Saskatoon which is 150 miles. Driving around the city was a little difficult, coming from the farm where there was not much traffic. But we managed. I remember one day, we drove up in front of the house. There was snow and I parked the car and dropped the keys in about a foot of snow. I had to go in and get some hot water and melt all around the door to find the keys. It was an interesting experience. Then there was a patch of ice in front of the car.

203

University was rather strange for me because I had never seen such sophisticated people and it was difficult to make friends because they weren't like the farm children at all. Most of them came from town. In fact the neighbors said to Dad, "What are you sending those girls to university for? They'll only get married. What a waste." But Mother insisted we finish whatever we were doing. Dorothy graduated a year before I did. I graduated in 1940, and she graduated a year before that in '39 and then she got a job with the government going around to Alberta, Manitoba, and Saskatchewan to teach home crafts, making cheese and growing gardens, and things of agriculture. How to get a bee hive going, and that sort of thing. The girls usually went to the town and they stayed there for perhaps two weeks and took this course on farm upgrading. Dorothy was a very good teacher. She enjoyed that and cooking. The young people enjoyed going to a farm school, although it was in the town.

I: What were your career goals?

G.O.: I did a degree in Home Economics and then I went to the Jubilee Hospital in Victoria to take my internship, which was where you worked for a year but you get your bed and board. I lived in the nurses' home. It was interesting, though a little strange but you get to know the other people in a residence like that. My mother and dad gave me $80.00. That was a lot of money, you know, in 1940, and that was all I had for 12 months, until I finished the internship. I was employed by the hospital after that, so I went on staff there for about four years.

I: And I remember you telling me that Emily Carr was there?

G.O.: Oh yes. She was a patient in the hospital. I guess about every two or three months she came in, and she, well, she was getting on you know. She died in '45 I think it was, and in '40, '41, and '42 I was the dietitian that had to go and visit her all the time. If I didn't go, she called down to the kitchen, "Where is the dietitian?" When I would get there she wouldn't tell me what she

wanted to eat, she would just talk about her monkey and living out with the Indians in the trailer. She had dogs. You know, she was an interesting old girl and nobody really appreciated her, which was a pity, and she knew that. She had just received the Governor General's Award for *Klee Wyck* and was at that time writing her *The Book of Small*. She was an odd girl, an odd lady you know. I don't think she ever wore anything but a muumuu, and her hair was done up in a net. She wasn't particular about her appearance, but she certainly had a good mind, and I feel badly now that I didn't take more time and talk to her, because she was terribly lonesome.

I: What was she in the hospital for?

G.O.: Heart. Every little while she would have to come to the hospital for her heart condition, and she finally died there in '45, but I had left by then. I am just ashamed because I didn't help her more.

I was at the Jubilee for four years and after I finished my interning and was on staff, I wanted to join the air force. I was coming over to Vancouver to see Flight Officer Jeffs, who looked after all the dietetic personnel, and when I told my husband this, then my boyfriend, who was in dentistry in Alberta, he said, "No, don't join up, it's not for you." For heaven's sakes, I believed him, which was too bad. I really would have liked to, because you went overseas for about six months, and I think it was interesting.

I: So mom, when you left Unity, you and dad graduated the same year. Did you have a sort of understanding that you would stay in touch. Did you consider him a boyfriend when you left?

G.O.: Oh yes, but I'm sure he went with every other girl in the district during the time he was growing up. I always figured I would marry him, but we were at different universities, he was in Saskatoon and I was out in Victoria interning. Anyway, we decided one year, 1943 in fact, that we would get married, so I went back to Unity to be married September 17th, '43. Then I had to go back to Jubilee Hospital because you couldn't leave a position in war

Excerpts from Some Interviews

205

time at that time. You had to find a replacement for yourself, otherwise you would have to stay. So I went back and worked for just about a year, and then went to Edmonton, where he was a student in dentistry, and there I was dietitian in charge of the cafeteria at the University of Alberta, which was nice. Then, after about a year and a half, I had to stop due to pregnancy, and we had you, our first daughter in Edmonton in 1944.

I: Tell me what dad was like at this early, early stage of the marriage. What was it that drew you together?

G.O.: Well, he was fun to be with, he was entertaining and was kind. If he had a few drinks then he would be very funny, which was too bad, because he kept on with that, but I admired him, and I think every girl in the district did. And he was attractive, I guess, and he also came from a family that we knew, lived seven miles from our house. They were a very stable family, I knew his two sisters and his mother and dad and his brother, so I thought it was a pretty safe thing to be married to someone from the district that knew me very well and also I knew him, I thought.

Some Suggested Interview Questions

When you arrive at a fork in the road, take it.
—YOGI BERRA

Each interview will follow its own path, concentrating on the special features, interests, and involvements of the teller—the things at the center of that person's life. It will also be shaped by the period in which the person lived. For example, if he or she lived through a war, you will want to ask questions about that. And, of course, the tone of the interview will be affected by the relationship between teller and interviewer. However, here are some questions that you might consider to make sure that you cover as many parts of the person's life as possible. They are only suggestions. Perhaps, choose the ones that are most important to you and then trust your own instincts and natural curiosity.

Before you even start asking questions, though, start the tape by identifying the teller by name, and the place, and date of the interview. Add your own name and your relationship with the teller. As with photographs, these details may be perfectly obvious to you now, but a clear identification is important because the tape will be kept

207

for the future. Then, quite casually, lead into some of the basic initial questions. If you appear relaxed and confident, the teller will quickly loosen up and overcome any natural nervousness.

Family background

Let's start by talking about your grandparents. What were their names?

When were they born? Where did they live?

Do you remember what they looked like?

What do you remember about them?

What did they do for a living?

What do you think was important to them in terms of values, philosophy, religion, politics, or ways of looking at the world?

Were you close to them?

Do you think you've inherited any characteristics from any of them?

Do you remember anything that would tell me a little about the kind of people they were?

(For as much detail as possible, ask about both sides of the teller's family: mother's mother, mother's father, father's mother, father's father. If you sense that the teller can reach back further and has information about other ancestors, ask about them as well.)

Tell me about the family your mother grew up in. Who were her brothers and sisters?

Did she grow up in the city or the country?

What do you know about her childhood?

What were the values in her family?

How was her family affected by the war? (Depending on when and where she lived.)

Did she ever tell you anything about her schooling, and what sorts of things interested her?

What did she do when she left school?

How did she meet your father? Did they ever tell you how they got married?

(Similar questions for father)

If the family emigrated from another country, why, when, and how?

Childhood

When and where were you born?

Where did you fit in the family among your brothers and sisters?

What are some of your early memories of your parents?

What did your mother look like?

Can you describe her personality?

What special skills or talents did she have?

Can you tell me about your relationship with your mother?

What sorts of things were important to her in the family?

How did she spend her time when you were growing up? Did she work outside the home?

Can you remember a time when she had to discipline you? What happened?

What things did you do together?

How did she deal with sadness or tragedy?

What moral or political values do you think she tried to teach you?

(Generally similar questions for father)

What were you like as a child?

What are some of the things that you remember about your brothers and sisters when you were a young child? Can you describe your relationship with them? What were they like as children?

Did you have pets? Tell me about them.

Who were your best friends?

What about toys? Any special favorites?

Do you remember any songs from your childhood, or stories that you were told?

What family activities do you remember from when you were little?

What was the neighborhood like where you grew up? Can you take me on an imaginary walk around it?

We carry the dead generations within us and pass them on to the future aboard our children. This keeps the people of the past alive long after we have taken them to the churchyard… "If there's one thing I can't stand, Russell, it's a quitter." Lord I can hear her still.

—Russell Baker

Did you take vacations? Where? Is there one that you remember particularly?

What about holidays and festivals—how would you celebrate them?

Did your family go to a church or a temple?

Were there any other people who were important to you in those early years?

Can you think of any smells that you associate with your childhood? What about sounds?

Are there any stories about when you were little that you remember or were told?

The world you grew up in is very different from today's world. Can you talk a little about how you traveled when you were small? What forms of entertainment were there? What were your clothes like?

Do you remember any special places? Any imaginary friends? Any fantasies you had about what would happen in the future?

First school years

What was your first school like?

Do you remember any of your teachers?

How do you think going to school was different then than it is now?

What about school friends?

What kind of student were you?

Were there any funny incidents that you recall about school?

Were you involved with sports, or clubs outside school at that time?

What did you want to be when you grew up?

How did you see yourself then? Were there ways in which you felt different from everyone else?

Was there any disruption in your life during those years? (Moving, a death, illness, war, etc.) How did you cope with it?

High school years

Which high school did you go to?

Which teachers made the greatest impression on you? Why?

What were your best subjects? Were there any you disliked?

Did you ever get into trouble at school or play pranks?

What about extra-curricular activities: music, sports, clubs?

Was adolescence a difficult time for you?

How would you describe yourself in your teen years?

When did you first discover girls (or boys)?

What do you remember about dating? Dances?

Was it easy for you to be with kids of the opposite sex? How did you feel about yourself as a teenager?

Do you remember any funny things that happened? Any embarrassing things?

Who were your friends at this time? What were they like? What would you do together?

Did you have any heroes when you were a teenager?

The teen years can be difficult ones for kids and parents. How were you getting along with your parents during this time?

What sorts of things became issues for you? How did you resolve them?

Did you have radically different values and ideals from your parents?

Do you feel your parents acted fairly when you had disagreements? Can you give an example?

What else was happening in the world when you were a teenager? How did it affect you?

Were you very aware of politics and world events?

Did you have a special high school graduation ceremony?

What did your family expect you to do after high school?

Where did you see your life going at this point? Did you have a clear ambition?

College

Where did you live when you were going to college?

How did you feel about leaving home? How difficult or easy was it for you to get established on your own?

Did you miss your family? How often did you see them?

Did you know how to cook? Was there any problem in looking after yourself?

How were you supporting yourself financially at this point?

What courses did you take at college?

Who were your friends (male and female), and what activities were you involved in?

College students are famous for playing pranks. Do you remember any?

How did college change you? What new ideas were you introduced to?

How long were you in college? Did you graduate?

What in general do you think you gained from your college experience?

Jobs

What was your first job? How did you get it? What did you have to do? What was the pay like?

What were working conditions like?

Was it a job just to make money, or was it something you were really interested in?

Where did you live?

Was this a good time of life for you?

During this period, what would make you happy? Unhappy?

Can you describe your contacts with your family at this time?

Did you have good friends?

How long did you work at your first job? Why did you leave?

What did you do next?

Friends

Did you make any special friends at this time?
What was special about them?
What activities did you do together?

Marriage

How did you meet your wife (or husband)?
Were you interested in him/her right away?
What attracted you to him/her? What was he/she doing at that time?
  What was he/she like?
What was your courtship like?
What do you remember about your wedding? Your honeymoon?
During the early days of your marriage, where did you live?
Was it hard to adjust to being married? What were some of the things
  you disagreed about?
How did you get by financially?
What did you see for yourselves for the future?

Family life

When was your first child born? How did you feel when you became
  a parent for the first time?
Were you confident about becoming a parent?
Why did you choose the name that you did?
Name the other children (if any), and tell when they were born.
  Why did you choose their names?
What were your children like as toddlers? As young children?
Do you have any favorite stories about them at that time?
What sorts of things would you do together as a family?
How did your ideas about child rearing differ from the way you were
  brought up?

213

Did you see your own parents differently when you became a parent?

What were they like as grandparents?

Were there differences between you and X (spouse) about how you dealt with the children? About discipline? About your expectations of the children?

What values did you try to teach your children?

How did you celebrate festivals? (Christmas, Hanukkah, Easter, Thanksgiving, Hallowe'en, other religious or cultural festivals)

Were you able to take vacations? Can you remember any that really stand out?

Did you move? Why and where? Was it a hard adjustment for any of you?

Can you tell me about your children as teenagers? Were they anything like you as a teen?

What was the most difficult part about being a parent? The most rewarding?

What were your hopes for your children when they were growing up?

How did they turn out?

How did you feel when they left home and made a life of their own?

Career

How did you make the decision to go into your line of work?

What about the work appealed to you?

Why do you think you were suited to that kind of work?

Can you sketch out the outline of your career, how it progressed over the years?

What have been the high points?

What do you think your major accomplishments and strengths were? Any weaknesses?

Do you remember any particular disappointments?

If so, how did they affect you?

Who were some of the people with whom you worked? Were they important to you?

Did you ever consider or make a complete change of career?

The rest of your life

Over the years, have you had any particular hobbies? Why does (did) it appeal to you?

Have you travelled a lot? Can you tell me about some of your adventures?

Do you have a favorite author? Why do that author's books interest you?

A favorite composer or musician? Artist?

What world events have affected you most closely?

What has been the hardest time of your life? How have you dealt with it?

How do you spend your time now?

Tell me about your grandchildren.

Do you have any particular stories about them?

How do you spend your time with them?

What do they add to your life?

In general

What sorts of things give you pleasure now? What makes you sad?

How do you deal with fears that you have?

How do you deal with loneliness?

Do you feel that the world now is a better place than it was when you were young? Why?

What concerns you about the way people are living nowadays?

What does doing this tape mean to you?

Looking ahead, what do you want to do in the next few years?

Are there any dreams that you want to pursue?

CHAPTER 14

Do you have any advice for your grandchildren?
What are your hopes for your grandchildren as they grow up?
Is there anything you'd like to add?

216

Forms for Classroom or Community Oral History Project

There are infinite possibilities for oral history projects that can be carried out in schools or communities, as we saw in Chapter 10. But it is always a good idea to be very clear what the purpose of the project is, and how the tapes will be used. To help you develop your own project, here are some samples of letters and forms that might be useful.

- sample letter to parents of students
- pre-interview form
- outline of questions
- release form

In order to make these forms meaningful, let us assume that we are doing a project with a sixth-grade class about immigration. We want find out something about the circumstances under which each family came to North America or to Belleville, where the school is located. Here is a sample letter to the parents of the students in your class.

Dear Parents:

During the next month and a half, our class will be engaged in an exciting project which we are calling *"Where in the world do we come from?"* We want to find out where each family came from, why they left their country or area of origin, how they came to Belleville, and what they found here.

Each student will be doing a tape recorded interview with a parent or grandparent on this topic. At the end of the month, there will be an evening to which you will be invited, at which time the students will tell the story of their family's immigration. We will also use a world map to identify exactly where each student's ancestral roots are.

Please don't hesitate to talk to me if you have any questions about this project. I'm looking forward to seeing you at our wind-up evening in six weeks.

Sincerely yours,

When the student has identified which family member he is going to interview, it is a good idea have a preliminary conversation with that person, and fill in a pre-interview form. This is some of the information that might give the student the basis for research he can do before the actual interview, and questions he can ask.

Sample Pre-interview Form

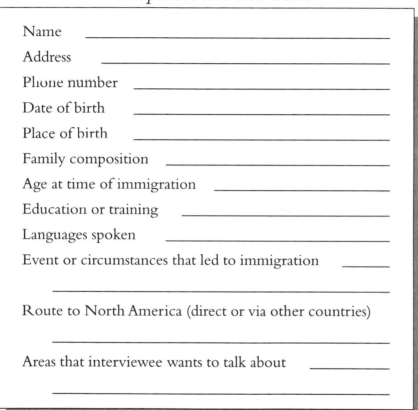

Name _____

Address _____

Phone number _____

Date of birth _____

Place of birth _____

Family composition _____

Age at time of immigration _____

Education or training _____

Languages spoken _____

Event or circumstances that led to immigration _____

_____

Route to North America (direct or via other countries)

_____

Areas that interviewee wants to talk about _____

_____

The outline of questions that the student will ask will cover the events of the immigration as well as stories, impressions, and more subjective reactions to those events. As a teacher, you can suggest some areas of discussion, but each interview will be unique, depending on the experiences of the teller. Let us assume that the teller is the father of the student, and came from China as a young man. Although there are a myriad of questions that could be asked, here are some suggestions:

Sample Outline

Can you describe your life in China before you decided to leave?

Why did you choose to leave China?

What were the social or political circumstances in China at that time?

How did your parents feel when you told them you wanted to leave?

What was it like to say good-bye to the friends you grew up with?

What did you expect to find in North America?

Were those expectations met?

Describe your voyage here.

What do you remember about your first day in North America?

How well did you speak English at that time?

Did you meet anyone during that time who was particularly helpful to you?

What was your plan in terms of studying or working?

How did you support yourself when you first came here?

Can you describe any occasions when you felt there was racism or discrimination?

How did you deal with that?

How easy was it to make friends?

What is important to you to retain in terms of your background?

How did you come to Belleville?

How has life changed for you since the day you first arrived?

Is there anything you'd like to add?

In Chapters 10 and 12 we spoke of the release form, the document which gets permission from the teller to use the tape of the interview in a specific way. Here is a sample:

Sample Tape Release

Name: (please print)

Subject to the conditions noted below, I release all rights to this recording to the Mountainview Elementary School in Belleville, where it may be used as part of the project *"Where in the World Do We Come From?"*

Conditions: none or

Signed: (interviewee)   (interviewer)

Address:

Phone Number:

Date:

COPYRIGHT
ACKNOWLEDGMENTS

Quotations

Foreword

p. xii   William S. Schneider. "Oral History Review," Fall 1987, p. 68.

p. xiv   Ruth Edmonds Hill, editor. *Black Women Oral History Project.* Westport, London, Meckler, 1991. Vol. 6, p.345.

N. Scott Momday. *Ancestral Voice.* Lincoln and London, University of Nebraska Press, 1989, p. xi.

p. xv   Ruth Edmonds Hill, editor. *Black Women Oral History Project.* Westport, London, Meckler, 1991. Vol. 6, p.351.

Chapter 1

Angela Sidney. From "Life Lived Like a Story," by Julie Cruikshank. UBC Press, Vancouver, BC, 1990, p. 36.

Chapter 2

Jane Austen. *Mansfield Park.* Bantam Books, first published 1814 Bantam Classics edition, 1983, p. 168.

Chapter 3

Elizabeth Stone. *Black Sheep and Kissing Cousins.* Penguin Books. New York, New York, 1988, p. 11.

Chapter 5

Margaret Atwood. *Cat's Eye.* McLelland and Stewart, Toronto, Ont., 1988, p. 3.

APPENDIX

Chapter 6
Johann Wolfgang von Goethe. *Goethe's World View: Presented in His Maxims and Reflections*, Ungar Publishing Co., 1958.

Chapter 7
Elie Wiesel,. *The Gates of the Forest.*

Chapter 8
Doris Lessing. "Under My Skin." *My Autobiography to 1849*, Vol. 1 Harper Perennial, 1995, p. 11.

Chapter 9
Margaret Laurence. *The Diviners.* McLelland and Stewart, 1974. Reprinted 1993, p. 14.

Chapter 12
Paulette Jiles. *Cousins.* Alfred A. Knopf, New York, 1991. p. 354.

Chapter 13
Robertson Davies. *Murther & Walking Spirits*, Penguin Books Canada, Toronto, Ont., 1991.

FURTHER READING

Family Stories
Black Sheep and Kissing Cousins; How Our Family Stories Shape Us,
   Elizabeth Stone, Penguin Books, New York, 1988.
*Family Tales, Family Wisdom; How to Gather the Stories of a Lifetime and
   Share Them with Your Family*, Robert U. Akaret with Daniel
   Klein, William Morrow & Co., New York, 1991.

Genealogy
Unpuzzling Your Past; A Basic Guide to Genealogy, Emily Anne
   Croom, Betterway Publications, Inc., White Hall, Virginia,
   1983.
*Your Family History: How to Use Oral History, Personal Family Archives
   and Public Documents to Discover Your Heritage*, Allan J. Lichtman,
   Vintage Books, New York, 1978.

Genograms
Genograms in Family Assessment, Monica McGoldrick and Randy
   Gerson, W.W. Norton & Co., New York, 1985.
*Genograms: The New Tool for Exploring the Personality, Career and Love
   Patterns You Inherit*, Emily Marlin, Contemporary Books,
   Chicago, 1989.
You Can Go Home Again; Reconnecting with Your Family, Monica Mc-
   Goldrick, W.W. Norton & Co., New York, 1995.

Interviewing Techniques
A Family Remembers, Paul McLaughlin, International Self-Counsel
   Press, North Vancouver, 1993.
Asking Questions, Paul McLaughlin, Self-Counsel Press, Vancouver,
   BC, 1986.

The Craft of Interviewing, John Brady, Vintage Books, New York, 1976.

Memoir Writing

Changing Memories Into Memoirs, Fanny-Maude Evans, Barnes & Noble Books, Harper & Row Publishers, New York, 1984.

Oral History

A Shared Authority; Essays on the Craft and Meaning of Oral and Public History, Michael Frisch, University of New York Press, Albany, 1990.

Envelopes of Sound; Six Practitioners Discuss the Method, Theory and Practice of Oral History and Oral Testimony, Ronald J. Grele, ed., Precedent Pub., Chicago, 1975.

Oral History: A Guide for Teachers (and Others), Thad Sitton, University of Texas Press, Austin, 1983.

The Voice of the Past: Oral History, Paul Thompson, Oxford University Press, Oxford, 1978.

Voices: A Guide to Oral History, Derek Reimer, ed., Provincial Archives of British Columbia, 1984.

Psychological Counseling

Family Ties That Bind: A Self-Help Guide to Change Through Family of Origin Therapy, Ronald W. Richardson, Self-Counsel Press, Vancouver, BC, 1986.

The Helping Interview, Alfred Benjamin, Houghton Mifflin Co., Boston, 1969.

INDEX